CAREERS FOR
HISTORY BUFFS
& Others Who Learn from the Past

Blythe Camenson

Second Edition

VGM Career Books

Chicago   New York   San Francisco   Lisbon   London   Madrid   Mexico City
Milan   New Delhi   San Juan   Seoul   Singapore   Sydney   Toronto

Library of Congress Cataloging-in-Publication Data

Camenson, Blythe.
    Careers for history buffs & others who learn from the past / Blythe Camenson.
        — 2nd ed.
        p. cm.   (VGM careers for you series)
        ISBN 0-658-02165-6 (alk. paper) -- ISBN 0-658-02168-0 (pbk. : alk. paper)
        1. United States—History—Vocational guidance.   2. Canada—History—
Vocational guidance.   3. History—Vocational guidance—United States.
4. History—Vocational guidance—Canada.   I. Title: Careers for history buffs
and others who learn from the past.   II. Title.   III. Series.

    E175 .C33   2002
    902′.373—dc21   2001026433

VGM Career Books

A Division of The McGraw·Hill Companies

1 2 3 4 5 6 7 8 9 0   LBM/LBM   1 0 9 8 7 6 5 4 3 2

ISBN 0-658-02165-6 (hardcover)
        0-658-02168-0 (paperback)

This book was set in Goudy Old Style by ImPrint Services
Printed and bound by Lake Book Manufacturing

This book is printed on acid-free paper.

To all the people who came
before us, for without them
we would have no history
and no avid interest to
consume us

Contents

A Word from the Author

Almost a decade ago, while interviewing the thirty or so professionals profiled in this book, I was struck again and again by the one thing all these diverse people had in common. From tour guides working for an hourly wage to chiefs and directors at the top of the salary scale, all of them unequivocally expressed love for the work they're doing.

At the time I thought it was rare to find so many people satisfied with their professions. Now, a decade later, in updating this book, I was able to track down all of the people featured within these pages. With the exception of one or two, most have stayed at the same jobs, still loving them as much every day as they did then. The few who have left their jobs have moved into self-employment but still maintain contact with their previous employers, several of them as consultants or individual contractors.

I thought so then, and I still feel that way now: there is something unique and wonderful about the field of history—and the people who enter it.

Salaries have hardly budged in the intervening years, and few if any of the history buffs within these pages have become famous, but they are all happy. My guess is if you pursue a career in this diverse field, you will be, too.

Acknowledgments

T he author would like to thank the following history lovers for providing information about their careers:

Don Albro
Former Director of Historic Sites
Joseph Smith Historic Center
Nauvoo, Illinois

Patricia Baker
Former Wardrobe and Textiles Manager
Plimoth Plantation
Plymouth, Massachusetts

Peter Benton
Restoration Architect
John Milner and Associates, Inc.
West Chester, Pennsylvania

Prudy Taylor Board
Publisher
Prudy's Press
Fort Myers, Florida

Jeff Donnelly
Volunteer Tour Guide
Miami Design Preservation League
Miami Beach, Florida

Tom Doyle
Carriage Tour Operator
Palmetto Carriage Works, Ltd.
Charleston, South Carolina

John Fleckner

Chief Archivist
National Museum of American
   History, Smithsonian Institution
Washington, D.C.

Mark Fortenberry

Former Curator of Structures
Nantucket Historical Association
Nantucket, Massachusetts

Jeremy Fried

Character Interpreter
Colonial Williamsburg Foundation
Williamsburg, Virginia

Tom Gerhardt

Interpretive Artisan: Cooper
Plimoth Plantation
Plymouth, Massachusetts

Hank Grasso

Exhibit Designer
National Museum of American
   History, Smithsonian Institution
Washington, D.C.

Kristin Kuckelman

Field Anthropologist
Crow Canyon Archaelogical Center
Cortez, Colorado

Kendra Lambert

Former Student Intern
National Museum of American
   History, Smithsonian Institution
Washington, D.C.

Michael Larsen

Literary Agent/Author
San Francisco, California

Antoinette Lee	Historian National Register of Historic Places Washington, D.C.
Deb Mason	Pottery Supervisor, Crafts Center Plimoth Plantation Plymouth, Massachusetts
Charles McGovern	Curator National Museum of American History, Smithsonian Institution Washington, D.C.
George Neary	Former Administrative Director/ Information Officer Miami Design Preservation League Miami Beach, Florida
Cookie O'Brien	Columnist Historic St. Augustine Preservation Board St. Augustine, Florida
Adam Perl	Antique Dealer Pastimes Ithaca, New York
Elizabeth Pomada	Literary Agent/Author San Francisco, California
Joel Pontz	Former Supervisor of Interpretive Artisans Plimoth Plantation Plymouth, Massachusetts

Mary Ptak   Vintage Clothing Specialist
                            Jezebel
                            Fort Lauderdale, Florida

Jim Ridolfi   Auctioneer
                            Aspon Trading Company
                            Troy, Pennsylvania

Roger and Mary   Former Proprietors
   Schmidt   18 Gardner Street Inn
                            Nantucket, Massachusetts

Jeremy Slavitz   Public Programs Coordinator
                            Nantucket Historical Association
                            Nantucket, Massachusetts

Carolyn Travers   Director of Research
                            Plimoth Plantation
                            Plymouth, Massachusetts

Gordie Wilson   Superintendent
                            Castillo de San Marcos National
                               Monument
                            St. Augustine, Florida

CHAPTER ONE

Jobs for History Buffs

Although the United States might be considered a young country, at least by the rest of the world's standards, it is still a land steeped in history. Throughout the country there are thousands of historic houses and public buildings, restored or reconstructed villages—even entire cities—to explore.

And always the melting pot, North America is ripe with relics of past visitors and civilizations—Vikings, early Native Americans, Spanish and French settlers, Pilgrims, Colonials, and pioneers of the Wild West, to name just a few.

Many history buffs don't limit their interests to North America. There's a whole world out there—Europe and Asia, Africa and South America, and Australia—with millennia of cultures and events to examine.

What Makes a History Buff?

History buffs are fascinated by events, places, and people from the past. There are armchair historians, devouring innumerable biographies and researched accounts, as well as hands-on types, out in the field digging for artifacts, exploring the lanes and roadways our ancestors once walked, or fighting to preserve historic buildings and monuments.

History buffs possess qualities as diverse as the areas of interests to explore. Some are thrilled by the discoveries of research or are collectors and catalogers by nature. They might enjoy working with their hands, recreating early American crafts with a potter's wheel or hand plane, or duplicating period clothing. To some, preserving and restoring the lines and structures of historic houses and buildings hold great interest.

Others love the smell of old books and paper and spend most of their time in libraries or government or private archives. Still others enjoy sharing their knowledge through talks and presentations or through the written word. They've found a niche working with the public as tour guides or information officers or writing articles and booklets for publication.

Among the traits history buffs do have in common are an insatiable curiosity and a love of the relics, events, people, and places of the past.

The Employment Outlook

Public interest in preserving our American heritage has grown tremendously in recent years. Where once settings in which history buffs could find employment were limited to a few museums and libraries, there are now thousands of new opportunities across the country. Every state has several departments devoted to different aspects of its local history. Most major cities, and even small towns, support a variety of historical societies and preservation boards. More and more historic buildings are nominated each year for inclusion on the National Register; many of these sites are operated as historic house museums open to the public.

New job titles have been added to the list once limited to curators and librarians. The field of history is now open to all sorts of professionals, including restoration specialists, designers, planners, financiers, audience advocates, information specialists, and many more.

Although the competition in some sectors is stiff, and funding always seems to lag behind public demand, a persistent history buff can get his or her foot in the door through volunteering or participating in a student internship.

Heaven-Sent Jobs for History Buffs

Job-hunting history buffs dream of finding a position where their skills and interests can be combined. Would any of these help-wanted ads send you racing to the post office to mail off your resume?

RESEARCHER   Author seeks experienced researcher for project documenting restored Victorian houses. Must be willing to travel.

TOUR GUIDE   Outgoing person with good communication skills needed to guide special-interest groups through American history museum in Washington, D.C.

POTTER   Wanted: fine-arts major familiar with or willing to learn seventeenth-century crafts techniques for demonstrating at living history museum.

DIG SITE ASSISTANT   Position open for energetic student or recent graduate at major archaeological dig site in New Mexico. Duties include cleaning and recording discovered artifacts.

INFORMATION OFFICER   Historic site preservation board has opening for officer to disseminate information to the public. Good writing skills necessary. Bilingual, Spanish/English a plus.

Requirements

Required qualifications vary depending on the job. Although many employers prefer their applicants to have a bachelor's or higher degree in history or a related field, not all do. Theater majors make excellent tour guides and character interpreters. Parks and recreation majors are a shoo-in with the National Park Service.

Many jobs discussed in this book don't require a college degree at all. In some situations, the following qualifications are more important: experience, extensive knowledge of a particular time period or region, the ability to communicate with diverse groups of people, and good writing and research skills.

Earnings

Salaries vary widely from position to position but are generally low, as are most pay scales for education-related fields. Factors such as the source of funding or the region of the country determine salary levels more than the complexity of the job or the level of the candidate's education and experience.

Some jobs pay only hourly wages; others follow the federal government's General Service (GS) scale. A tour guide might earn $6 to $10 an hour, an information officer perhaps $25,000 to $30,000 a year, a restoration architect $30,000 to $40,000.

Most jobs provide benefits such as health insurance. But all those interviewed on the pages to come stressed that financial rewards were not the main reason, or even a consideration, in pursuing their chosen professions. The low pay is far outweighed by the satisfaction of doing work they love.

Choosing a Profession

With so many areas of history to explore, how do you know which avenue would be right for you? Take a look at the chart that follows. Find your interests and skills, then look across to identify career options. You'll see that many of the job titles combine more than one interest. A short description of some of these jobs follows the chart; more in-depth discussions will be found in the chapters to come.

Interests and Skills	Job Titles
Old houses	Restoration Architect, Architectural Historian, Curator of Structures, Preservationist, Curator, Exhibit Designer, Historic Interiors Specialist
Working with your hands	Restoration Architect, Curator of Structures, Archaeologist, Artisan, Archivist, Costumer, Antique Dealer, Refinisher, Exhibit Designer
Finding out information	Historian, Researcher, Archaeologist, Archivist, Genealogist, Curator
Working with the public	Character Interpreter, Tour Guide, Information Officer, Park Ranger, Historic Inn Operator, Public Relations Representative, Educator, Auctioneer
Writing	Information Officer, Public Relations Representative, Curator, Archaeologist
Working outdoors	Archaeologist, Restoration Architect, Character Interpreter, Curator of Structures, Park Ranger, Auctioneer

Job categories are as varied as the locations. The following paragraphs give a brief overview of the dozens of jobs discussed in this book.

Jobs for Historians

The term *historian* covers a large range of career options and job settings. In general, historians study, assess, and interpret the past to determine what happened and why. They examine court documents, diaries, letters, and newspaper accounts; they interview individuals and study archaeological and artifactual evidence. They conduct research, write, teach, evaluate, and make recommendations.

Historians work in schools and universities, in libraries and museums, in government offices and private enterprises.

Jobs in Living History Museums

Do you have a good memory (and good vision)? Do you like to pore through old documents researching lives of America's ancestors? How about a flair for improvisation and the dramatic? Can you think fast on your feet? Or work with your hands? These qualities, and more, could land you a job as a researcher, character interpreter, or craft worker at Colonial Williamsburg or Plimoth Plantation, two of the many living history museums throughout the country.

Jobs with the National Park Service

Most people picture park rangers for the National Park Service dressed in snappy uniforms, battling blazing forest fires with a trusty companion, Smokey the Bear, standing by. And while many rangers are concerned with fire prevention, nature, and conservation, there is another category of ranger that would be of interest to history buffs. Interpretation park rangers, both men and women, work at the more than two hundred historic sites and national monuments throughout the country. This division of rangers is devoted to preserving and explaining the past.

Jobs in History Museums

History museums offer a wide range of positions, from directors and curators to educators and designers. Depending upon the position, responsibilities could include collecting, preserving, restoring, displaying, explaining, and guarding.

Jobs in Architectural History and Restoration

Lovers of the architectural styles and structures of the past are moved to study them, restore and renovate, reproduce, or preserve and protect them. They often work with their hands, creating drawings or lifting beams and sanding wood trim.

Jobs with Preservation Boards and Historical Societies

People who work on preservation boards and in historical societies enjoy teamwork, serving on committees, and educating the public—and they are not afraid to fight for a cause they believe in. Through the work of dedicated preservationists across the country, thousands of historic buildings, even entire districts, have been saved from the wrecking ball. Many of these sites have gone on to achieve national recognition.

Jobs in Archaeology

Do you dream of traveling to Egypt or Israel, to Peru or Turkey? Can you pay attention to detail and perform delicate, painstaking tasks? As an archaeologist or assistant, your work could take you around the world, literally uncovering the past, one grain of sand at a time.

Jobs in Genealogy

Genealogists act as detectives to the past, tracing missing persons, filling in the holes in family histories. They interview older family members; visit courthouses, cemeteries, and libraries; and spend hours poring through diaries, old newspaper accounts, marriage licenses, and birth and death certificates.

Jobs for Writers and Photographers

If you have a talent for writing, or know how to handle a camera, you can make your own presentation, sharing through words and pictures various events, places, and artifacts of historical interest. Writers and photographers produce books and pamphlets, postcards and posters.

The Self-Employed History Buff

Want to be your own boss? There are many businesses and sidelines into which a history buff can venture, including the following examples: running a historic inn; dealing in antiques; creating, promoting, and operating your own tour company; restoring and selling vintage clothing. The list is limited only by your imagination.

Other Jobs for History Buffs

The "ologies"—anthropology, paleontology, and geology—as well as education, art history, and landscape archaeology are just a few more career paths that dedicated history buffs with an academic leaning can investigate.

The Job Hunt

Although many history buffs are able to find employment in their own hometowns—in local historical societies or historic house museums—chances are you'll have to relocate to broaden your opportunities. If you have a spot in mind where you'd like to work, a phone call or an introductory letter or E-mail sent with your resume is a good way to start. If you would like some more ideas on possible locations, there are several directories listed in the coming chapters and in the appendices that can lead you to interesting destinations.

Since many sites are state or federally operated, you might have to obtain a special application through state or federal offices. Some private employers, however, such as the Colonial Williamsburg Foundation, expect job hopefuls to apply in person. The foundation regularly posts openings and operates a job hot line with recorded messages.

Many historical organizations and professional associations produce monthly or quarterly newsletters with job listings and upcoming internships and fellowships. Some key addresses, as well as suggested further readings, have been provided for you throughout the following chapters and in the appendices.

Don't forget the Internet, which, these days, has become one of the premier resources for job hunting. Fire up any search engine and enter key words such as *history, jobs, museums, curators*, and so on. A well-defined search will bring you to some interesting and helpful websites.

Also visit the websites of the professional associations listed in Appendix A. Many of these websites offer specific career information and list job openings.

Living History Museums
Making History Come Alive

A living history museum is a vibrant, active village, town, or city where the day-to-day life of a particular time period has been authentically recreated. Once you step through the gates, you leave the present behind. The houses and public buildings are restored originals or thoroughly researched reproductions. Interiors are outfitted with period furniture, cookware, bed linens, and tablecloths. Peek under a bed and you might even find a two-hundred- or three-hundred-year-old mousetrap.

Residents wear the clothing of the day and discuss their dreams and concerns with visitors as they go about their daily tasks. If you were to stop a costumed gentleman passing by and ask where the nearest McDonald's is, he wouldn't seem to have any idea what you were talking about—unless he thought to direct you to a neighbor's farm. He might even do so using the dialect of his home country.

Colonial Williamsburg in Virginia and Plimoth Plantation in Massachusetts are just two examples of living history museums. The addresses and websites of several others can be found in Appendix B.

These large enterprises offer employment for professional and entry-level workers in a wide variety of categories. These include, but are not limited to, character interpreters, presenters, costumers, and researchers.

Many sites are state or federally funded, and still more receive their support through admission tickets and private donations. Falling into this latter category is Williamsburg, a painstakingly restored colonial-era village.

Close-Up: Colonial Williamsburg

Visitors to Colonial Williamsburg meet historic figures, witness events, and participate in the daily lives of the people who helped bring about American independence.

For eighty-one years, from 1699 to 1780 (though only die-hard history buffs need remember the dates), Williamsburg was the thriving capital of Virginia, one of the original thirteen American colonies. After the American Revolution, when the capital was moved to Richmond, Williamsburg began a decline that lasted 146 years. It became a sleepy southern town with crumbling roads and buildings, overgrown gardens, and only a distant memory of patriots and prosperity.

In 1926, with his love of American history and a belief that anything is possible, John D. Rockefeller Jr. began the Colonial Williamsburg restoration project to return this once-important city to its former glory.

Now, after more than sixty years of work, eighty-eight original eighteenth-century and early nineteenth-century structures have been completely restored, and more than five hundred others have been reconstructed on original foundations—but only after extensive archaeological and historical investigation.

The principal thoroughfare in Williamsburg is the Duke of Gloucester Street, which began as nothing more than a winding horse path flanked by a tavern and a few shops and houses. Then, in 1693, with the establishment of the College of William and Mary (North America's second-oldest university, Harvard being the oldest) at the western end and the impressive capitol building at the far eastern end, the street was widened and became the busy center of daily activity. Today it is closed to traffic, though an occasional horse-drawn carriage or stagecoach clatters by. Eighteenth-century shops and houses still stand, shaded by beautiful old trees lining the hard-packed dirt walkways.

These buildings are not just empty symbols of a bygone era, however. Many of the homes shelter permanent residents—employees of the Colonial Williamsburg Foundation—or act as inns to house the many visitors who come every year.

Those that are open to the public are filled with the same artifacts, activities, and people that made up daily life in colonial times.

Character Interpreter

The most visible living history museum employees are the scores of men and women decked out in authentic period costumes. They can be found waiting inside the buildings or walking through the grounds, and although they might seem to be there just for decoration—or "photo opportunities," as they are sometimes called—most are trained researchers, actors, and presenters. A select group of these staff members use "first person" interpretation or role playing to explain about their places in history. They are called *character interpreters* or *people of the past*. They are in actuality skilled social historians who have researched early residents and assumed their roles.

In Williamsburg, you can follow Mrs. Powell about town as this eighteenth-century housewife does her errands, or visit the Powell House and speak with Mr. Powell, the prominent Williamsburg builder.

You can spend the afternoon in the capitol yard listening to colonial gentlemen discussing events of the day or converse with Mr. Samuel Henley, an eighteenth-century professor at the

College of William and Mary, and learn about the values and traditions of his time. You can even eavesdrop on young gentlemen as they prepare for college and share their expectations and concerns for the future.

Children can join a costumed interpreter to explore the interaction of colonial family life, youth apprenticeships, education, work, and leisure time.

Adam Waterford, a free black cooper, and young Charles, the son of the Powell family's cook, are also on hand for a glimpse into the colonial African-American experience.

At Plimoth Plantation you can listen to seventeenth-century Goodwife Cook plan her day or share tidbits of gossip with Governor Bradford's sister-in-law. John Alden is there, making barrels in his one-room cottage or helping other villagers erect a new house. Not too far away, seventeenth-century sailors swab the decks or repair the lines on the *Mayflower II*, while passengers discuss their worries about surviving the first winter in the New World.

What It's Like to Be a Character Interpreter

Jeremy Fried, in addition to his position as manager of character interpreters at Williamsburg, has been interpreting the role of James Hubard, a colonial lawyer, off and on for more than ten years. Jeremy explains his job:

"My character spends most of his time in chambers, a fair-sized room in the courthouse, with a table in the middle seating twelve people. I sit down with a law book and quill and paper, and people come in and chat. But I don't work from a prepared script—that's what makes this form of interpretation different from other forms of living history.

"A character interpreter, often with the help of our various research departments, examines the life of an eighteenth-century person by reading available documentation—personal letters,

letters to the editor, newspapers. From this we can make inferences about their lives and what their beliefs were. As accurately as possible, we portray their ideas, social knowledge, and political opinions.

"Visitors ask questions about how 'I' became a lawyer, about my family, about life in general in the eighteenth century. I've had people stay with me for one-and-a-half to two hours. This gets to be a bit of a challenge to stay in character. But I enjoy it."

Qualifications

Jeremy Fried stresses that the most important qualifications an applicant should possess are the ability to communicate with people, a pleasing personality, and an inquisitive mind.

These requirements generally hold true for all living history museums throughout the country.

Jeremy Fried further explains: "Of course, the foundation prefers people with a history major, but the flip side is, unless you've done your master's thesis on colonial Virginian society, you're still going to have to do the research. You could have only a GED but still be able to formulate new ideas and coordinate information.

"We have a number of folks with history degrees, but we also have a retired florist and a former petty officer in the navy. It's a mixed bag of backgrounds. I have a degree in theater from the American Academy of Dramatic Arts in New York."

In addition, candidates would have to be the appropriate age and sex for a particular character they might be asked to play.

Jeremy points out one other qualification: "An applicant would have to be willing to accept a pretty low pay range."

Salaries

A full-time entry-level character interpreter earns only an hourly wage, from minimum wage to around $10, which varies with experience. But although it's an hourly wage, employees are given full benefits. Most contracts are for a ten-month period. A percentage of employees are laid off for two months during the winter, then rehired.

Offsetting the low salaries, Jeremy Fried points out, is that the people really enjoy working for the foundation.

"It's a nice work environment," Fried says. "The biggest stress is being hospitable to folks on vacation, and that's not a bad situation."

Salaries vary from site to site, of course, but most generally follow the same range offered in Williamsburg.

Hours

Most full-time employees put in an eight-hour day. At least four of those hours are spent in the characters' natural environment in chambers, in class at the college, or in their shops or homes. The rest of the time is spent moving around town, chatting with visitors, becoming a photo opportunity.

Ample time during the week is also allocated for research or to produce facsimile newspapers in the winter months.

Character interpreters at Plimoth Plantation attend to all the necessary tasks to keep the village thriving. They work in the fields, care for the farm animals (which have been back bred to resemble breeds from three hundred years ago), and build new houses or repair existing ones.

Advancement

Opportunities occasionally come up to move into more administrative roles. A national association of interpreters has been newly formed to let people know that interpreting history is a highly specialized skill.

"Right now, though," Jeremy Fried admits, "the only way to advance is to get out of interpreting and into management."

How to Apply

A quick telephone call or letter will have an application on its way to you. Some sites even have job lines to tell you what positions are currently available. See Appendix B for more information.

Presenter

Jobs for presenters are much more numerous throughout the country than are character interpretation positions. Presenters differ from character interpreters in that most work from prepared scripts. Here, acting ability is more important than research and ad-libbing skills.

Presenters generally reenact moments from history—a court scene, the Boston Tea Party, a fife-and-drum corps march—or other aspects of life in the historic site's particular period.

Sometimes, because enough information is not available for a particular place or people—the native people in seventeenth-century Plymouth, for example—a character interpreter would not be able to authentically take on a first-person role. Then presenters would explain to visitors what is known about the time in the third person. Presenters usually perform outfitted in authentic costumes.

Salaries for presenters are generally low, and employment can often be seasonal, but the rewards of discussing your favorite place or time in history often compensate for the downsides.

Costumer

Most living history museums employ professional costumers to keep their character interpreters and presenters outfitted in authentic period clothing. Costumers generally work behind the scenes, reproducing the apparel the average inhabitant would have worn.

What It's Like to Be a Costumer at Plimoth Plantation

Patricia Baker was wardrobe and textiles manager and is now an occasional consultant at Plimoth Plantation, a living history museum that has recreated the year 1627, seven years after the arrival of the *Mayflower* at Plymouth Rock. Her office and work space occupied a section of a converted dairy barn on the grounds of the museum. The atmosphere was that of a cozy living room with lots of shelves, fabrics draped here and there, sewing machines and rocking chairs, a large cutting table, garment racks, and a radio. Patricia discusses her former job:

"The department I worked for makes clothes that are common to what the middle class would have worn. It provides interpreters with enough clothing so they can dress authentically from the skin out. They don't even have to wear modern underwear if they don't want to.

"The basic undergarment for both men and women is a shift. It's a long, linen, T-shaped garment that reaches to the knees. Over that, the men wear breeches and a doublet, a close-fitting jacket that comes to just above the waist. The breeches are tied into the jacket by laces.

"Women wear a plain corset over the shift. It gives them a smooth, cone-shaped look. Next come a number of petticoats and skirts and a padded roll to enhance their hips. Waistlines are raised and meet in a point.

"The costumers use wool and linen and a little cotton, all naturally dyed, and try to duplicate the same materials used in the seventeenth century, as well as the same construction techniques. Much of the sewing is done by hand.

"They also make all the household furnishings that are used for display in the various exhibits. These are the seventeenth-century equivalents to what we have in the twentieth century: sheets, pillowcases (called *pillow beres*), feather and straw beds, paneled bed curtains, tablecloths, napkins, and cupboard cloths.

"Maintaining and repairing existing costumes and furnishings are also part of the duties, as well as conducting as much research as possible to keep the creations accurate for the particular time period.

"Because there are so few surviving garments—conditions were very harsh in those early years—costumers look to different sources: paintings, engravings, wood cuts, written descriptions, wills, inventories, diaries, and plays.

"They also study the few remaining garments on display in different museums through our extensive slide collection of styles and techniques. Most of those museums are in England, the Victoria and Albert or the Museum of Costumes in Bath, for example. The clothing seems to have had a better survival rate over there."

Background

Patricia graduated from the Massachusetts College of Art in 1976 with a bachelor of fine arts degree in crafts. Her concentration was in fabrics and fibers.

She immediately began work at Plimoth Plantation as a character interpreter. She joined the wardrobe department in 1985 and became its head the following year. She now works with the Costume Society of America and occasionally serves as a consultant for Plimoth Plantation.

How to Get Started

The wardrobe department at Plimoth Plantation is a small one, currently employing only four workers. Other larger living history museums, such as Colonial Williamsburg, need more people. A good way to get a foot in the door is to apply for an apprenticeship, internship, or work-study position.

Salaries

A new graduate just starting out could expect an annual salary in the $20,000 to $30,000 range, depending on the location and available funding.

The Historic Trades

Most living history museums employ skilled artisans to demonstrate early crafts and trades. Some of these artisans perform in the first person, playing the role of a particular character of the time. Others wear twentieth-century clothing and discuss their crafts from a modern perspective.

In the stores and workshops lining the Duke of Gloucester and Francis Streets in Colonial Williamsburg, you will find harness makers, milliners, tailors, needleworkers, silversmiths, apothecaries, candle makers, bookbinders, printers, and wig makers. In the Pilgrim Village and Crafts Center at Plimoth Plantation, there are coopers, blacksmiths, joiners (cabinet makers), potters, and basket makers and weavers.

In addition to giving demonstrations, artisans often produce many of the items used on display in the various exhibits. This includes the furniture, cookware, and even sometimes the actual buildings.

Interpretive Artisans at Plimoth Plantation

Most of the items the Pilgrims used in 1627 were brought with them on the *Mayflower* or imported later. Because the Pilgrim

Village at Plimoth Plantation is time-specific to the year 1627, only those crafts that were practiced then are demonstrated there. In addition to their principal occupation as farmers, 1627 Pilgrims were coopers, blacksmiths, thatchers, and house builders. The interpretive artisans perform in costume and play the role of a designated Pilgrim documented to have lived in Plymouth during that year.

What It's Like to Be a Cooper at Plimoth Plantation

Tom Gerhardt interprets the character of one of the most famous Pilgrims, John Alden, a cooper who worked both inside a one-room cottage he shared with his wife and two children and outside in the adjoining yard. Tom talks about his job:

"I make barrels and other different-sized wooden containers, such as buckets and churns, while answering visitors' questions about life in seventeenth-century Plymouth.

"Although in Europe you could still find people practicing the craft as it once was done, there are only a few barrel makers in this country. Wooden barrels are made mostly for the wine and spirits industry, but now it's a mechanized craft using power tools and machinery. The finished product is the same as the old craft, but the method is different. We practice the craft as it was done in the 1600s, using only hand tools.

"In addition to my duties as an interpretive cooper, I am also responsible for general woodworking. I am one of several Pilgrims building a new house on the grounds.

"What I enjoy most about Plimoth Plantation is that there are a number of very creative and talented people here. If you're willing to do the work, you can learn a good deal for yourself, while at the same time you're educating the visitors.

"There are so many people who will help you—you can be inspired by what they're doing; and you have the time to explore and develop your skills."

Background

Tom Gerhardt's interest in history began as a small child. His father was a volunteer in charge of a small museum in Virginia, and he took the family on vacations all over the country visiting other museums. It was on one of these trips Tom first discovered Plimoth Plantation.

Later, Tom took a few courses under a master cooper in Portsmouth, New Hampshire, and went to college for a couple of years, studying general liberal arts and theater. He worked in the technical end of theater for a while but decided he wanted a change. Since he'd always been interested in the recreation of history, in 1985 he came back to Plimoth Plantation and applied for a job as an interpreter. He has been working there ever since.

What It's Like to Be a Joiner at Plimoth Plantation

Plimoth Plantation also operates a Crafts Center where other seventeenth-century crafts are demonstrated. Potters, joiners, basket makers, weavers, and a gift shop share space in a converted carriage house. Artisans in the Crafts Center wear twentieth-century clothing and discuss their work from a modern viewpoint.

Joel Pontz was the supervisor of all interpretive artisans at Plimoth Plantation as well as character interpreter for a farmer, John Adams. He also demonstrated his joinery skills in the Crafts Center. He now does custom woodworking and occasionally completes contract work for Plimoth Plantation. Joel describes his former job:

"I stepped back and forth between the seventeenth and the twentieth centuries. Several days a week I was in costume in the village as John Adams, picking my share of rutabagas or building small animal shelters or fences. On the other days I was in modern clothing in the Crafts Center, demonstrating joinery.

"Joiners were the principal furniture makers of the period, in the age before cabinetry. We used different kinds of saws and edged hand tools, such as axes, planes, gimlets, and augers, rather than power tools. If we wanted to reproduce the right texture or style, we had to be purists about it.

"In the Crafts Center, in front of the public or behind the scenes, we made furniture for the village—large cupboards, bedsteads, chairs, mousetraps, and children's toys. We didn't want to demonstrate any crafts in the village section of the museum that weren't practiced at the time. It would be anachronistic."

Background

Joel Pontz grew up nearby and started at Plimoth Plantation as a volunteer Pilgrim after school and on weekends. In 1973, he became a full-time character interpreter. He learned his joinery skill on site, from the other staff members and the research department.

"I hated woodworking in school," Joel admits. "It wasn't until I started working at the plantation, using hand tools and trying to decipher how things were made, that it became actually interesting for me. The historical aspect of it was what fascinated me. If it were just doing straight carpentry, I probably wouldn't have stayed with it."

How to Get Started

Joel advises taking a few courses in historic trades or historic preservation. "But," he cautions, "the skills we need are particular to Plimoth Plantation. Outside courses would be painted with such a broad brush, but what's done at Plimoth Plantation is very focused on a particular group of people in a very short time span.

"The best qualification would be a lot of hand-tool work. The tools haven't changed that much over the centuries. Try taking a tree and make a table or a chair from it. That's the best way to learn the art."

Because of limited budgets and a low turnover, openings are rare. However, there is an occasional internship as well as a volunteer program that could help you get your foot in the door.

What It's Like to Be a Potter at Plimoth Plantation

In the Crafts Center at Plimoth Plantation, four potters demonstrate seventeenth-century throwing techniques, though only one potter is on duty at a time. They also make all the pieces that are used in the village by the interpreters. During the winter months when the museum is closed to visitors, the potters make enough items to replenish the stock.

Deb Mason has her own home studio, where she teaches pottery classes, does commission work, and makes pieces for display at various galleries. She also spends several hours a week in the Crafts Center and is the supervisor of the other potters. Deb talks about her job:

"In the Crafts Center, we don't claim to be seventeenth-century people because pottery wasn't done in the village in 1627. But because of this, we have an advantage. We can talk to visitors in a way that's totally different from the interpreters. A visitor might go to the village, then come back to the Crafts Center to ask a question that the seventeenth-century interpreters couldn't answer. The interpreters have to speak as though they are Pilgrims. They wouldn't have any knowledge beyond 1627.

"For now we are working with twentieth-century equipment, though we are discussing the possibility of going back in time, using a kick wheel and a wood-burning stove. The electric wheels we use now might make throwing look faster and easier than it was in the seventeenth century, but the techniques are still very much the same.

"The difference is we have to make only period pieces, and there some of the difficulties come in. For example, we're trying to find the right clay bodies to work with. We have a few original pieces on display to study, and you can see the clay color and texture. We've been experimenting, trying to develop clay bodies that are close to the original.

"That's been fairly successful, but we're having a tough time with glazes. They used a lot of lead back then. In fact, most every glaze was lead-based. Because we sell the pieces we make in the gift shop and they're also used in the village every day, we've been trying to get away from lead. It's hard to come up with glazes that have the same shine and the same colors; lead has a very typical look. We're using a ground glass that melts at a low temperature, which is a characteristic of lead, and produces similar results.

"We make ointment pots that held salves and other healing lotions, apothecary jars, bowls, porringers for porridge, oil lamps, candlesticks, and pipkins—little cooking pots with a side handle and three legs on the bottom.

"We also make a lot of three-handled cups. Pilgrims usually shared their eating implements. The cups are funny-looking things—a popular item in the craft shop.

"Back then the pottery was hastily thrown. There's a real earthy quality to the pieces. Their perception of what was beautiful and what was utilitarian was different. What they strove for was extremely rough by today's standards.

"My biggest problem is remembering not to throw too well. The advantage to that, though, for potters wanting to work here, is that a high degree of skill is not necessary."

Background

Deb Mason earned her bachelor's degree in art with a major in ceramics in 1973 from Bennington College in Vermont. She taught ceramics full-time for thirteen years at a private school and was the head of the art department her last few years there. She joined the staff at Plimoth Plantation in 1992.

Salaries

Salaries for craft workers differ depending on whether they are full-time or part-time. Part-timers are paid hourly.

Researcher

Researchers form the backbone behind every living history museum. Without their efforts, the ability to recreate authentic period characters, to accurately restore historic buildings, or to reproduce a facsimile of daily life would be an impossible task.

What It's Like to Be a Researcher at Plimoth Plantation

Carolyn Travers is director of research at Plimoth Plantation. She talks about her job:

"We have four sites at Plimoth Plantation: the 1627 Pilgrim Village; the *Mayflower II*; Hobbamock's Homesite, a Wampanohg Indian site; and the Carriage House Crafts Center. We research anything we need for our program, from what is the period attitude toward toads and how a character felt about being her husband's third wife to the correct way to cook a particular dish or some obscure point of Calvinist theology.

"The women are more difficult to research than the men because there is less documented information on them. You are forced into recreating a more typical persona than the actual character, sort of a generic portrayal. In general, we research the life and genealogical background and social history for all the characters we portray.

"In our research, we use a variety of sources—court records and genealogical research done by professional genealogists, such as the General Society of Mayflower Descendants, or writers for the *American Genealogist* or other genealogy periodicals.

"We also have researchers in other departments. For example, the authenticity of buildings and structures is done more by our curatorial department."

Background

Carolyn attended Earlham College, a small Quaker school in Richmond, Indiana, where she earned a bachelor's degree in fine arts with a concentration in history. She went on to Simmons Graduate School of Library and Information Science in Boston and graduated in 1981 with a master's degree in library and information science with a concentration in research methods.

Carolyn grew up in Plymouth and started work at the age of fourteen as a part-time Pilgrim. After she finished her master's degree, she returned to Plimoth Plantation as a researcher.

Qualifications

Carolyn points out that researching is a competitive field, and that a higher degree, in history or library science with a research methods concentration, is necessary.

A candidate is not expected to have a general body of knowledge about the specific time period, but he or she must have strong research skills, talent, and experience.

Salaries

New graduates might begin with yearly salaries in the high teens or low twenties. "You don't do it for the money," Carolyn stresses. "There are a lot of psychological payments. One of the satisfactions is to be able to change someone's mind about the stereotypes surrounding early colonists."

Researchers can find work in a variety of other settings as well: university archaeology and history departments, preservation boards, libraries and archives, government offices, and history museums.

Other Jobs at Living History Museums

The following is a list of other job categories found in living history museums. Many are discussed in detail in later chapters.

Architecture	Educational Programs
Archaeology	Information
Business Affairs	Personnel
Building and Grounds Maintenance	Public Relations
Collections Management	Sales
Curatorship	Security
Development and Membership	Visitor Services

The National Park Service
Interpreting Our National Treasures

T he National Park Service, a bureau under the U.S. Department of the Interior, administers more than 160 natural and recreational areas across the country, including the Grand Canyon, Yellowstone National Park, and Lake Mead.

Another two hundred sites of cultural and historic significance fall under the park service's jurisdiction and offer numerous employment opportunities of interest to history buffs.

Most history-related jobs are located in the mid-Atlantic, Southeast, and national capital regions; most archaeology-related positions are in the West and Southwest. The various sites encompass battlefields, national monuments, historical and military parks, forts, and memorials.

Because most sites are not located near major cities, serious candidates must, for the most part, be prepared to relocate. Housing may or may not be provided, depending upon the site and your position.

The National Park Service Website

Visit the National Park Service's website at www.nps.gov. By clicking on Links to the Past and then the drop-down box, you'll find another link to job and volunteer opportunities.

There you'll find some general information on National Park Service careers and application processes. There are also convenient links to the Office of Personnel Management and to the Volunteers in Parks (VIP) program.

The website also includes a guide to volunteer and archaeological fieldwork opportunities both in and out of the National Park Service, with information on special archaeological weeks in specific states.

Visit www.cr.nps.gov/museum to learn about the National Park Service's Museum Management Program, including events, exhibits, and opportunities.

Park Ranger (Interpretation)

The National Park Service hires three categories of park rangers (usually on a seasonal basis): enforcement, general, and interpretation. Most history buffs apply for positions in the interpretation category.

Duties vary greatly from position to position and site to site, but rangers in the interpretation division are usually responsible for developing and presenting programs that explain a park's historic, cultural, or archaeological features. This is done through talks, demonstrations, and guided walking tours.

Rangers also sit at information desks, provide visitor services, or participate in conservation or restoration projects. Entry-level employees might also collect fees, provide first aid, and operate audiovisual equipment.

Career Potential

Depending upon qualifications, park rangers begin their service at various grades. From the entry, rangers may move through the ranks to become district rangers, park managers, and staff specialists in interpretation, resource management, park planning, and related areas.

At upper levels, rangers' responsibilities and independence increase as their influence covers more staff and area. Upper-level managers in the Park Service are recruited primarily for their managerial capabilities.

Competition exists for park ranger positions in all grade levels. The starting salary level for summer ranger hires with college degrees is a GS-4 ($18,687); permanent ranger hires are GS-5 ($20,908) to GS-9 ($31,680), depending on college degrees and experience.

Education and Earnings

In determining a candidate's eligibility for employment, and at which salary level he or she would be placed, the National Park Service weighs several factors. In essence, those with the least experience or education will begin at the lowest federal government salary grade of GS-2. But the requirements for that grade are only six months of experience in related work or a high school diploma or its equivalent.

The more relevant work experience or education, the higher the salary level. For example, GS-4 requires eighteen months of general experience in park operations or in related fields and six months of specialized experience—or one ninety-day season as a seasonal park ranger at the GS-3 level.

Completion of two academic years of college may be substituted for experience if the course work covers social science, history, archaeology, parks and recreation management, or other related disciplines.

Close-Up: St. Augustine—America's Oldest City

From an aerial vantage point or entering from the south across the Bridge of Lions (named for the Spanish explorer Ponce de León), St. Augustine, Florida, America's Oldest City, resembles a European burg, a medieval hamlet. Fairy-tale castles with spires and turrets rise above the roofs of gingerbread-trimmed dollhouses. Horse-drawn carriages, stone walls, city gates, and a coquina block fort add to the fanciful effect.

Reputedly one of the oldest roadways in the oldest city in the country, St. George Street was fully restored in the mid-1970s. On either side of the narrow promenade, signs adorn vintage buildings proclaiming the Oldest Wooden School House, built during the first Spanish occupation before the American Revolution, the Oldest Pharmacy, and the Oldest Store, with a collection of more than one hundred thousand of yesterday's mementos.

St. Augustine's Oldest House is one of the most-studied and best-documented houses in the United States. It was originally built with palm thatchings covering a crude structure of logs and boards, then restored after a fire in 1702 with coquina walls and tapia flooring (a mixture of lime, shell, and sand). The house provides a record of life in St. Augustine for more than four hundred years. Archaeologists, through digs and research, have shown continuous occupancy of the site dating from the early 1600s to the present day—in spite of raids, looting, and fire.

Nearby, the Authentic Old Jail, listed in the National Register of Historic Places, contains the original weapons used in crimes and offers an interesting courtyard display. The building, with living quarters for the sheriff and his family, served the county until 1953.

South of the Old City Gate is St. Augustine's Spanish Quarter. In this living history museum are restored homes and gardens more than 250 years old. Guides and artisans dressed in period clothing recreate the daily lifestyle, giving visitors an inside look at life for eighteenth-century soldiers and settlers.

Castillo de San Marcos National Monument, built by the Spanish between 1672 and 1695 and now run by the National Park Service, is dubbed America's Oldest Fort. It took more than fifty years after Ponce de León claimed *La Florida* for Spain to establish a permanent settlement in St. Augustine. The early Spaniards had many clashes with colonialists in neighboring Georgia and North and South Carolina. St. Augustine was burned to the ground twice. The fort was finally constructed to secure the city.

Lacking brick-making materials, the Spanish used blocks of coquina, a native shell stone quarried locally across the bay on Anastasia Island. Softer than brick, it helped the fort withstand numerous attacks, its walls absorbing the impact of iron cannon balls rather than shattering the way brick would.

The coquina tends to break off when touched, and portions of the fort have been eroding away. The damage is irreparable; a mortar substitute can be used to patch up the surface here and there, but park rangers warn visitors not to lean against the walls.

The fort raised different flags above its walls many times during the years, through wartime and peace, through treaties, trades, and negotiations, but in 1821 it changed hands for the last time when the United States acquired Florida from Spain.

The fort is also significant in that it houses what claim to be the nation's oldest toilets.

Further Reading

America's First City: St. Augustine's Historic Neighborhoods, by Karen Harvey, illustrated by Nina McGuire (Tailored Tours Publications).

What It's Like to Be a Park Ranger at Castillo de San Marcos

Gordie Wilson graduated college in 1977 with a degree in parks and recreation and immediately began working for the National Park Service. Today, in addition to his post as superintendent of Castillo de San Marcos National Monument, he is also in charge of nearby Fort Matanzas National Monument. Gordie talks about the duties of a park ranger:

"There really is no such thing as a typical day. Duties are varied, and there is always the unexpected. A park ranger might begin the day sitting at the ticket booth collecting fees, then go inside the fort to give a two-hour presentation to visitors, explaining the fort's history. Later, costumed park rangers set off the cannons in a daily display, while others ensure that would-be treasure hunters are not defacing the property with shovels and metal detectors.

"If a visitor has a heart attack, which is not a rare occurrence, then trained park rangers will administer CPR or other forms of first aid. A park ranger must be prepared to take on a variety of duties."

Getting Your Foot in the Door of the National Park Service

"Competition for jobs, especially at the most well-known sites, can be fierce," Gordie Wilson explains, "but the National Park Service employs a huge permanent staff, and this is supplemented tenfold by an essential seasonal workforce during peak visitation periods.

"The best way for a newcomer to break in is to start off with seasonal employment during school breaks. With a couple of summer seasons under your belt, the doors will open more easily for permanent employment."

And, because of Office of Personnel Management regulations, veterans of the U.S. armed forces have a decided advantage. Depending upon their experience, they may be given preference among applicants.

Summer Employment Opportunities

The Historic American Buildings Survey/Historic American Engineering Record (HABS/HAER), a division of the National Park Service, seeks applications from qualified individuals for summer employment documenting historic sites and structures of architectural, landscape, and technological significance throughout the country.

Duties involve on-site fieldwork and preparation of measured and interpretive drawings and written historical reports for the HABS/HAER Collection at the Prints and Photographs Division of the Library of Congress. Projects last twelve weeks, beginning in May and June.

Salaries range from entry-level positions at $4,500 to more senior positions at approximately $8,500 for the summer, depending on job responsibility, locality of the project, and level of experience.

Visit the website at www.cr.nps.gov/habshaer for more detailed information on how to apply.

Applying for Temporary Employment

Recruitment for summer employment begins September 1, with a January 15 deadline. Some sites, such as Death Valley or Everglades National Park, also have a busy winter season. The winter recruitment period is June 1 through July 15. The application requirements are as follows:

1. Applicants may apply for employment year-round.

2. Positions covered under this system are

   a. Park Ranger (Interpretation) GS-5 and GS-7

   b. Park Ranger (General) GS-5 and GS-7

   c. Park Ranger (Law Enforcement) GS-5 and GS-7

   d. Park Guide GS-4, GS-5, and GS-6

   e. Visitor Use Assistant GS-4, GS-5, and GS-6

   f. Biological Technician GS-4, GS-5, GS-6, and GS-7

3. All applications must be postmarked before the closing date of the announcement.

4. Applicants may apply to any and all park opportunities.

5. Applicants may update their applications at any time, day or night, as long as it is before the closing date of the announcement.

6. Applicants only have to answer the *core* questions section of the application once.

7. Applicants *must* answer the *specialty* questions for each position to which they are applying.

8. Go to www.sep.nps.gov to find an on-line temporary employment application.

Applications for seasonal employment with the National Park Service can be obtained through the Office of Personnel Management or by writing to:

U.S. Department of the Interior
National Park Service, Seasonal Employment Unit
P.O. Box 37127
Washington, DC 20013

You may also contact one of the ten regional offices of the National Park Service for local information. These addresses are listed in Appendix C.

Historian

In addition to park ranger positions, the National Park Service has another category called, simply, *historian*. Duties involve conducting research and producing inventories and reports on specific sites, structures, and technical processes.

Historians also work with the National Register of Historic Places, which is a branch of the Interagency Resources Division administered by the National Park Service.

The National Register of Historic Places

The National Register of Historic Places is the United States' official list of national resources worthy of preservation. Part of a national program, the National Register of Historic Places supports public and private efforts to identify, evaluate, and protect America's historic and archaeological resources.

The National Register includes all historic areas in the National Park System, National Historic Landmarks designated by the secretary of the interior, and properties such as historic districts, sites, buildings, structures, and objects significant in American history, architecture, archaeology, engineering, and culture.

There are more than two thousand nominations put forward each year; the vast majority meet all eligibility requirements and are entered in the National Register. The following chart shows a few interesting listings.

Property	Significance
The Moulin Rouge Hotel in Las Vegas, Nevada	Of exceptional importance in the history of integration: first club built (1955) to cater to an integrated audience.
The Ma Rainey House, home to Gertrude Pridgett "Ma" Rainey, nicknamed Mother of the Blues, Columbus, Georgia	For her contribution to the world of music.
The Luber School in Stone County in the Arkansas Ozarks	A one-room stone building remarkable as a monument to educational reforms both in Arkansas and nationally.
The ruins of "Galloping Gertie," a collapsed suspension bridge submerged in Puget Sound near Tacoma, Washington	The bridge's failure ushered in new developments in bridge design and aerodynamics.
The Eric Ellis Soderholtz Cottage, home to the noted potter and photographer, West Guildsboro, Maine	Built by the artist, it's one of the state's most distinctive Arts and Crafts cottages and an important example of craftsman architecture in rural America.

Admission to the National Register of Historic Places brings national recognition and various tax benefits—and federal grants for historic preservation when funds are available. Nominations usually begin on the local and state level, by individuals and agencies, then are submitted to the National Register of Historic Places for final review.

Being a Historian with the National Register

The National Register of Historic Places employs about twelve full-time professional historians, architectural historians, and archaeologists. Historian Antoinette Lee has been with the National Register since November of 1989. Antoinette discusses her job:

"I coordinate our National Register program. We produce a lot of technical information on evaluating properties for the National Register. I handle public accessibility by promoting the National Register's Starter Kit through advertisements. The kit is helpful to people considering nominating a property. I also issue press releases on new monthly listings.

"All the historians are assigned different regions in the country; I am responsible for the register's programs in the western states. I evaluate the nominations to the register that come in, then admit them if they're eligible.

"We participate in different workshops and seminars and get out in the field occasionally to meet people on the front line of historic preservation at the state and local levels."

Background

Antoinette's interest in history was largely influenced by her grandmother, who in the 1920s and 1930s worked toward the preservation of Pullman, Illinois—George Pullman's railway community.

Antoinette has more than twenty years of experience in the field. She earned a bachelor's degree in history at the University of Pennsylvania and her doctorate in American civilization from George Washington University in Washington, D.C.

During the bicentennial era in the 1970s, she did a lot of free-lance research work for various historians, architectural historians, and preservationists who were involved in major studies commemorating the 1976 bicentennial. One of her projects was a history of state capitol buildings. In the late 1970s and early 1980s, she worked as education coordinator for the National Trust for Historic Preservation, which is a private, nonprofit preservation organization.

After that, she worked for eight years as a private consultant in historic preservation. When a friend showed her the announcement for the position of historian with the National Register of Historic Places, Antoinette applied by filling out the Standard Form 171 and was selected.

What It Takes to Be a Historian

A candidate for the position of historian should be willing to serve the public and should have an understanding of history at all its levels—national, state, and local. It is also important to be aware of the preservation needs of the public and to be able to help people in achieving their goals.

To quality for a historian position, which merits a federal government rating of GS-5 through GS-15, applicants must have at least a bachelor's degree in architectural history, history of technology, American civilization, historic preservation, or a related field. A graduate degree is preferred. Having several years worth of field experience is also important in order to be able to adequately evaluate nominated properties.

For current salary information in these grades, check with the Office of Personnel Management (there are offices in most major cities) or with any federal agency.

Getting a Foot in the Door

Paid internships are available through the National Council for Preservation Education, but the number of internships offered is relatively small. There are generally numerous job and internship opportunities at the state and local levels. You can start your investigations at your local library. For more information call or write:

National Register of Historic Places
National Park Service
1849 C Street NW
NC400
Washington, DC 20240
www.cr.nps.gov/nr

CHAPTER FOUR

History Museums
Displaying the Past

Nothing makes history come more alive than to hold a piece of it in your hands. From acquiring collections and preserving them to explaining and displaying them, history buffs in history museums have the chance to work with every aspect of the relics and other forms of physical evidence of the past.

There are thousands of history museums across the country. They are housed in purpose-built structures or in historic buildings and homes that are open to the public. Many are large enterprises employing scores of professionals to handle day-to-day operations. Other museums are small and operate with only a handful of employees and dedicated volunteers.

The larger the museum, the more specialized an employee's duties are. Professionals in midsize or small museums must be willing to take on a variety of tasks. However, knowledge of or familiarity with all areas of museum functions, in addition to a strong background in a particular discipline, are important qualifications for any staff member.

Along with the proper educational achievements, the American Association of Museums (AAM) suggests these additional qualifications for museum personnel:

A museum professional should be expected to have a familiarity with the history, goals, and functions of museums; a knowledge of and commitment to the AAM statement on ethics; and a willingness to improve skills by study and by attendance at training sessions, seminars, and professional conferences.

Dedication, integrity, diplomacy, and a commitment to thoroughness and accuracy are demanded of all museum professionals. The ability to communicate orally and in writing and to work constructively with associates is essential.

An awareness of legal issues affecting museums and the ability to prepare and interpret budgets and grant applications are required of all positions. Additional knowledge, skills, and abilities such as a second language, typing and word processing, and familiarity with the museum's community and its resources may be required for certain positions and are always beneficial and desirable.

The AAM has identified dozens of direct and museum-related career categories. Several of those of interest to history lovers are examined here, along with the expected requirements for levels of education, experience, knowledge, abilities, and skills.

Collections Manager

The collections manager supervises, numbers, catalogs, and stores the specimens within each division of the museum.

EDUCATION REQUIREMENTS   An undergraduate degree in the area of the museum's specialization is the minimum requirement. An advanced degree in museum studies with a concentration in a specific discipline is recommended.

EXPERIENCE   Most museums prefer candidates to have at least three years of experience in a museum registration department or in a position in which the main duties are the technical aspects of handling, storage, preservation, and cataloging.

KNOWLEDGE AND SKILLS   Collections managers need knowledge of information management techniques, the ability to accurately identify objects within the museum's collection, and knowledge of security practices and environmental controls.

Curator

Curators are specialists in a particular academic discipline relevant to a museum's collections. They are generally responsible for the care and interpretation of all objects and specimens on loan or belonging to the museum, and they are fully knowledgeable about each object's history and importance.

Depending upon the museum and its areas of interest, curators can work with textiles and costumes, paintings, memorabilia, historic structures, crafts, furniture, coins, or a variety of other historically significant items.

EDUCATION REQUIREMENTS   A curator would normally possess an advanced degree with a concentration in an area related to the museum's collections.

EXPERIENCE   Three years of experience in a museum or related educational or research facility would usually be required before a candidate could advance to a full curatorial position.

KNOWLEDGE AND SKILLS   The curator must have the ability to explain and interpret the collection to the public and be familiar with the techniques of selection, evaluation, preservation, restoration, and exhibition of the museum's collection.

Director

A museum director must have specialized knowledge of the museum's collections and be responsible for acquisitions, preservation, research, and presentation. A director also must be familiar with making policies, handling funding and budgets, supervising staff, and coordinating museum activities.

EDUCATION REQUIREMENTS   An advanced degree in the area of the museum's specialty is required, with specific course work in museum administration.

EXPERIENCE   A museum director needs three years or more of management experience in a museum or related institution.

KNOWLEDGE AND SKILLS   A director should have specialized knowledge of at least one area of the museum's collections or in the management of the particular type of museum. His or her area of expertise must also include implementing policies and financial planning.

Educator

An educator's main function is to enhance public awareness of and access to the museum's collections. To do this, an educator designs and implements programs encompassing a variety of media and techniques and arranges for special events, workshops, and teacher training programs. In addition, an educator might train docents and tour guides and might have other supervisory and administrative duties.

EDUCATION REQUIREMENTS   The job requires an advanced degree in education, museum education, or one of the museum's specialty areas.

EXPERIENCE   Two years of experience in a museum education department or other related facility are needed.

KNOWLEDGE AND SKILLS   An educator needs the ability to prepare material for publications and exhibitions, skills in oral and written communication, and knowledge of school systems' curricula and research techniques.

Exhibit Designer

Exhibit designers work closely with curatorial and educational personnel to convey ideas through permanent or temporary exhibits. They use drawings, scale models, special lighting, and other techniques. An exhibit designer can have administrative responsibilities and may supervise the production of exhibits.

EDUCATION REQUIREMENTS   A degree or certification in graphic or industrial design, commercial art or communications arts, architecture, interior design, or studio arts is needed.

EXPERIENCE   Designers need to gain experience in exhibition design and related construction work with wood, metal, or plastics. A portfolio of past and current work is necessary.

KNOWLEDGE AND SKILLS   Skills in conceptualizing exhibit designs, creating mechanical drawings, making refined aesthetic judgments, and supervising exhibit installation are essential.

Salaries

According to reports in the *Occupational Outlook Handbook*, median annual earnings of curators, museum technicians, and conservators are approximately $32,000. The middle 50 percent earns between $23,000 and $44,000. The lowest 10 percent earns less than $16,340, and the highest 10 percent earns more than $63,580.

Earnings of curators vary considerably by type and size of employer and often by specialty. Average salaries in the federal government, for example, are usually higher than those in religious organizations. Salaries of curators in large, well-funded museums can be several times higher than those in small ones.

The average annual salary for all museum curators in the federal government in nonsupervisory, supervisory, and managerial positions is about $59,000. Museum specialists and technicians average around $40,400.

The Smithsonian Institution

When most Americans think about spending a day at the mall, they've got shopping 'til they drop on their minds. But residents of and seasoned visitors to Washington, D.C., know that the Mall, located between the U.S. Capitol and the Washington Monument, is a nicely manicured strip of land housing the nine museums of the Smithsonian Institution complex. The Smithsonian also has six other museums and galleries—two are located in New York—as well as the National Zoological Park. The museums are named here:

Anacostia Museum

Arthur M. Sackler Gallery

Arts and Industries Building

Cooper Hewitt Museum (New York)

Freer Gallery of Art

Hirshhorn Museum and Sculpture Garden

National Air and Space Museum

National Museum of African Art

National Museum of American Art

National Museum of American History

National Museum of the American Indian (New York, Maryland, and a new facility under construction on the Mall)

National Museum of Natural History

National Portrait Gallery

Renwick Gallery

Smithsonian Institution Building (the Castle)

The chief executive officer of the Smithsonian is given the title of secretary. The institution is governed by a board of regents that, by law, is composed of the vice president of the United States, the chief justice of the United States, three members of the Senate, three members of the House of Representatives, and nine private citizens. Traditionally, the chief justice of the United States has served as chancellor of the museum.

The Castle houses the Smithsonian's central administration offices. Each individual museum has its own director and staff.

The National Museum of American History, which is part of the Smithsonian Institution complex on the National Mall, is devoted to the exhibition, care, and study of artifacts that reflect the experience of the American people. The museum receives more than five million visitors a year. It has the responsibility for preserving the more than sixteen million objects it has acquired during the last century, and it has more than 430 employees on staff.

What It's Like to Be a Curator at the Museum of American History

Charles McGovern is supervisor of the American History museum's division of Community Life, overseeing a group of technicians, specialists, collection-based researchers, curators, and support staff. He is also a curator, responsible for Twentieth-Century Consumerism and Popular Culture. This department covers the history of entertainment, leisure, recreation, and commerce.

The exhibits within this department are probably the most popular and the most well known. Visitors to the museum come to view Judy Garland's ruby slippers from the *Wizard of Oz*; Caroll O'Connor's well-worn chair used by his character, Archie Bunker, on "All in the Family"; or ventriloquist Edgar Bergen's famous wooden dummy, Charlie McCarthy.

Charles's interest in cultural history began at an early age. He watched a lot of television and listened to the radio and participated in the mass popular culture in the 1960s. His father and mother told him about the times when they were growing up, sharing with him stories about the early days of radio. When Charles got to high school and read books his teachers recommended, he realized that Babe Ruth and Laurel and Hardy and the Marx brothers, personalities he cared very deeply about, were as much a part of history as Calvin Coolidge or the First World War. Charles talks about his job:

"Part of my profession as a historian is to be a decoder or an explainer, to go back into the heads and the lives and the beliefs of our ancestors. And here, we try to do that respectfully, understanding the world as they saw it. As we do that, we see how culture reflects the times, the fears and ideals and problems of a given society. You cannot look at certain creations of our popular culture without seeing those kinds of elements in them.

"As a curator, I am responsible for the creation and maintenance of the collections in my subject area. I document the history of the everyday life of American people. The major outline for my job puts me in charge of building collections, developing exhibitions, conducting research, writing, public service, public speaking, and being a graduate advisor to eleven research fellows.

"Specifically, my job is divided into three parts: acquisitions, which means acquiring new objects and exhibits for the museum; exhibiting and interpreting; and research.

"The collections I am responsible for include a lot of the things related to the history of American entertainment: a hat that Jimmy Durante used in his stage appearances; Ann Miller's tap shoes; Howdy Doody; Mr. Moose, Bunny Rabbit, and the Grandfather clock from Captain Kangaroo; the suit of armor worn by Francis X. Bushman in the original 1936 movie *Ben Hur*; Carol Burnett's char lady costume; Mister Rogers's sweater; Harrison Ford's Indiana Jones outfit (his leather jacket and hat); Tom Selleck's ring from 'Magnum, P.I.' and his Hawaiian shirt and baseball cap; old 78 rpm records; movie posters; and comic books. We also look for collections that give us insight into American consumerism and commerce. We have the bonnet that was worn by the woman who posed for the Sun-Maid raisin box; a huge collection of turn-of-the-century advertising, marketing, and packaging items from the Hills Bros. Coffee Company; and a collection of memorabilia from World's Fairs from 1851 to 1988.

"To build our collections, we depend largely on people donating items. In fact, almost everything has been donated. We have very little money in our acquisitions budget. We can't compete in a very inflated market with the galleries and people who deal with 'collectibles.' People must be willing to donate, so we look for people who either don't need the money or get the point of what we're trying to do.

"Sometimes we're not able to accept everything that is being offered. Someone called once and wanted to donate Charlie Chaplin's cane. But first, how do I know it was his cane? It's impossible to document that. And second, Chaplin probably went through thousands of canes. Those bamboo things snapped very easily. Something like that we couldn't take.

"And although I must be familiar with every piece's history, the range and variety of items I am responsible for is staggering. It's not as if I were a curator of painting where I'm trained in oils and brush techniques. Once in a while I have to confer with an appraiser or dealer to determine authenticity.

"Once a donation has been accepted, we can never promise that it will go on display. Less than 2 percent of our collection is on display at any given time; the rest is kept in storage. Although some exhibits, such as the ruby slippers or Archie's chair, are permanent, others rotate.

"Part of my job is to decide what gets exhibited, what gets stored, what is rotated. And to care for all the items, to make sure they don't deteriorate, we need to remove even permanent exhibits from time to time. People travel a long way expecting to see a certain item, and if it's not on display they're usually upset. They don't realize they should check with us first if they're coming to see something in particular. We took Charlie McCarthy off to clean him one day, and within a half an hour we had three phone calls saying where was Charlie McCarthy?

"The exhibiting side of my job is really a team effort. Exhibit designers work with curators to decide *how* an item should be displayed. The designer is responsible for the layout of objects and text and graphics and props. A conservator, someone who takes care of the actual repair or maintenance of an object, would be responsible for the 'prescription'—'This piece needs to be lit with not more than thirty foot-candles,' for example.

"But I feel that research is really my first duty. All the collecting and exhibiting doesn't mean anything unless you have something to say. You have to figure out first what point you're making. Our point is the showing of everyday life of the American people, and for earlier times that's something that has to be researched. Of course, you do research to support the things you already have in your collection, but the research also helps you to determine what you should be out there collecting."

Background

Charles studied at Swarthmore College in Pennsylvania and finished in 1980 with a bachelor's degree, with honors, in history.
He immediately began graduate school at Harvard and earned
his master's degree in history in 1983 and his doctorate in American civilization in 1993.

During that time, Charles taught history at Harvard, and then
from 1986 through 1987 he served at the Smithsonian as a
research fellow. In 1988 he became a full-time curator.

The Smithsonian as a Training Ground

Every year, the Smithsonian awards dozens of research fellowships, providing funding to doctoral candidates and access to
museum collections. To be hired as a curator, candidates must
have a doctorate or be almost finished with it. Entry-level positions include technicians and specialists and research-related
jobs. Paid internships and volunteer positions are usually available and a good way to get a foot in the door.

Charles points out that jobs for curators at the Smithsonian
seldom become available. But because the Smithsonian has a certain reputation and skill in training, it's a good place to gain a
foundation and then go out to other areas or institutions for
work. An internship at the Smithsonian will go a long way in
securing employment elsewhere. He believes that because of the
Smithsonian's size, sometimes really interesting work gets done in
smaller museums with a more fixed mission.

Salaries

A beginning curator who has almost completed a doctorate
would come in somewhere in the low $30,000s. The next jump
would be to the high $30,000s. Staff at the Smithsonian are
employees of the federal government and follow the GS scale.

What It's Like to Be an Exhibit Designer at the Museum of American History

Many small and even midsize institutions do not have room in their budgets for a specialist exhibit designer. In a situation such as that, one or two people, the director or the curator, might perform the functions of an exhibit designer in addition to the duties of their own specialties. Or, in some cases, the museum will contract with an outside firm for exhibit design work.

The Smithsonian Institution, a large operation, employs more than twenty exhibit designers and assistants; five of those designers work specifically for the National Museum of American History.

Hank Grasso was a senior exhibit designer working in all of the different departments within the National Museum of American History. Hank came to the Smithsonian in 1990 as a visual information specialist, the government's position for an exhibit designer. He generally functioned as part of a team of professionals including curators, collections managers, conservators, scriptwriters, audience advocates—or educators, as they are most often known—and project managers. He came on board specifically to work with the American Encounters Show, the museum's Columbus quincentenary presentation, dealing with five hundred years of history in America.

Hank has also worked on the designs for the "Working People of Philadelphia" in the Life in America exhibit, Science in American Life, the East Broadtop Railroad, Manufactured Weather, and Feed Bags as Fashion, a popular exhibit on an unusual fashion trend. Hank discusses the process of exhibit design:

"If you have a thousand images and ten square feet of space, you need to come up with a vehicle that will allow those images to be displayed. For example, you can compress them into a video disk or a series of slide presentations or storyboards. We look at the information we're wanting to convey and then translate it visually, keeping an eye to spatial allocations.

"There are two distinct models you can follow. With the traditional model, the cast of characters involved stay in very rigid roles: the curator passes abstract ideas to the designer, who then translates them into a physical presentation. The curator is responsible for content, ideas, and the written word; the designer is responsible for the environment, esthetics, and graphic design.

"A more modern approach is called a collaborative exhibition development, involving a team of professionals working together. We worked this way when we were creating the American Encounters show, a permanent exhibit at the Smithsonian. We created design tools so all parts of the team could understand each other. We could look over each other's shoulders and know what we were seeing."

Putting an Exhibit Together

These are just a few of the many steps a collaborative team follows when working on a new exhibit:

1. Listen to ideas and identify interpretive goals. Why are we telling this story? What is the most important message we want to convey?

2. Look at the available space and create a floor plan.

3. Combine steps 1 and 2 by prioritizing ideas and looking at the elements that will hold the exhibit together.

4. Decide how it will be done—presentation vehicles, techniques, and technology.

5. Choose the objects and images that will best tell the story.

6. Make a scale model that renders all the individual objects, labels, and graphic images.

7. Translate design control drawings, sets of drawings that have to do with the general contracting and building of spaces and with the making of exhibit parts.

8. Write the script and labels for the exhibit.

9. Begin the competitive bid process for general contracting.

10. Construct a full-scale model.

11. Conduct audience research. How does the audience react? Does the audience understand the materials and ideas being presented?

12. Do final construction.

13. Handle promotional and outreach elements.

Background

Hank attended Denison University, a small liberal arts school in Ohio, from 1972 to 1974. During his two years there, he had a chance to get a good overview of the various courses and decide what he wanted to pursue. He then transferred to Penn State and studied in the wood products division, specializing in wood as an art medium, looking at both its aesthetic and structural uses. He also combined his study of wood products with courses in the architecture department, including drafting and drawing, and graduated in 1976 with a bachelor's degree in interdisciplinary studies. He later went back to school at Pratt Institute in New York and took graduate courses to increase his conceptualization skills and learn more about different fabricating techniques.

Between his time at Penn State and Pratt, Hank worked for a couple of different private design firms that were contracted by various museums. While building up his portfolio, Hank had an opportunity to work on exhibit designs for the John F. Kennedy

Library in Boston, the Basketball Hall of Fame, the Bowling Hall of Fame, the New York Historical Society, the United Nations, the Metropolitan Museum of Art, the Frederick Douglas Place, and the Buffalo Bill Historical Center.

In 1996, Hank Grasso started his own firm, Planning and Design, Inc., in Kensington, Maryland. He occasionally does contract work for the Smithsonian.

Getting on the Right Path

Today there are three main educational preparation choices for someone wishing to pursue a career as an exhibit designer.

1. Institutions such as Pratt or Parsons School of Design offer good courses in industrial, graphic, and commercial design.

2. Some universities can provide a liberal arts education combined with certain skill courses.

3. A candidate can attend a professional program in a field such as architecture.

Hank suggests that once your theoretical education is completed, so much more of what is still out there to study can be learned through internships and working for diverse design firms, which also gives the new exhibit designer a chance to build a portfolio, an important tool for moving on to the next position.

Salaries

Exhibit designers work directly in museums or for private firms on contract with museums. Not surprisingly, salaries paid by the private sector often top those a museum can pay, even if the designer is doing the same work in the same institution.

Annual salaries for entry-level workers can range from $17,000 to $23,000 and are several thousand dollars higher in a private firm. An exhibit designer with more than ten years of experience could expect to earn somewhere in the $40,000s to $50,000s.

Notes from a Student Intern's Journal

In addition to his other duties, exhibit designer Hank Grasso was often responsible for the supervision of interns. Kendra Lambert, from Auburn University in Alabama, was one of his students. She spent her last summer in college learning about graphic design at the National Museum of American History. Here are some of the notes she kept on her experiences there:

"Attended staff meetings for American Encounters. Met curators, designers, educators, and the team writer along with other interns working on the project. At these meetings each team member's thoughts were expressed concerning deadlines, progress to date, and objectives. Interaction is clearly important to working as a team.

"I helped build a prototype of two cases, Pueblo and Spanish missions, within the exhibit. Maps were enlarged from photocopies and mounted on foam core. Time lines were set on the Macintosh using a PageMaker program, then cut and mounted to be used on a larger scale. The purpose of the prototype was to test audience reaction to typefaces used. Hank wanted to find out if people are sensitive to these subtleties in type and if symbols help some people break down information. Curators also reworded some of the labels. It meant more work for the design department, but it was important to have an accurate representation of the cases.

"I learned to draw objects to scale working on the Feed Bags as Fashion case. I was responsible for the title logo. Hank wanted to work from the original stencil face from an actual feed bag. It became too complex to create letterforms when we had no reference.

"During Feed Bags, I got to work in the Exhibit Production Lab. I helped set type for labels, I observed the process for silk screening, I positioned the text on panels. It was great to be part of production! And within hours of opening the exhibit, the press was there. It was great—and such a huge audience response. People loved it.

"I have learned that designing exhibits requires a person who is flexible to schedule the meetings that are a part of working in a team and still complete the required drawing and model work.

"It is important for an exhibit designer to make an exhibit more accessible to the public, who can then begin to learn what ideas the curators are attempting to communicate. I have observed that an exhibit designer needs a graphic artist to make decisions about type treatment, type placement, logo development and creating graphics.

"One of my goals this summer was to arrange portfolio reviews in the Washington, D.C., area and meet professional designers. Hank looked at my design portfolio and immediately recommended I speak with a colleague. This interview taught me a lot! I also had the opportunity to meet with the former director of design at the museum.

"I am scheduling an appointment with the assistant of exhibition design at the National Gallery. I have recorded suggestions from these reviews that will enable me to improve my portfolio and decide on a direction for my senior project. It has been valuable also in developing interviewing skills. I feet more confident about my work and have a clearer idea of what aspect of design I will follow as a career as a result of this internship."

Kendra Lambert graduated from Auburn University in December 1991 then went to work at the Birmingham Museum of Art as a publications designer, designing all the printed promotional pieces that the museum uses, such as invitations, newsletters, posters, and T-shirts. Kendra's goal is to attend a master of fine arts program in design history.

A Small Museum

Nauvoo, Illinois, is a historic city on the banks of the Mississippi River, near the point where Iowa, Missouri, and Illinois meet. Fairly isolated, Nauvoo is 260 miles south of Chicago and about 170 miles north of St. Louis.

Originally it had been a Sac and Fox Indian village, named Quashquema, for their chief. When Mormon founder Joseph Smith arrived in 1839, he called the site Nauvoo, from the old Hebrew word meaning "beautiful place."

The town is laid out like a mini-Williamsburg, with beautiful gardens and more than two dozen restored homes and shops open to the public. Early crafts have been given a second life, and skilled artisans give daily demonstrations. Most of the staff, including the director, the guides, and caretakers, live on-site. In fact, the year-round population of Nauvoo numbers only eleven hundred, and most of these residents work for either of the two main churches that share ownership of the town.

The Church of Jesus Christ of Latter-Day Saints (the Mormons), whose headquarters is in Salt Lake City, Utah, owns and operates the visitors center on the north side of town, as well as many other neighboring properties.

The Joseph Smith Historic Center on the south side of town is operated by the Reorganized Church of Latter-Day Saints, whose headquarters is in Independence, Missouri. The Joseph Smith Historic Center has a visitors center that houses a greeting gallery, two theaters, and a small museum room displaying artifacts of the Smith family. There is also a library containing rare books of the period, along with reference books on the restoration and reconstruction of historic buildings and artifacts.

Visitors to the Joseph Smith Historic Center also tour the Joseph Smith Homestead, whose log cabin portion was built around 1803; the 1842 Mansion House; the Smith family cemetery; and the Joseph Smith Red Brick Store, which was reconstructed in 1979.

What It's Like to Be a Director at the Joseph Smith Historic Center

Don Albro was director of historic sites at the Joseph Smith Historic Center until his retirement in 2000. He feels he was chosen for this position because of his long relationship with the church (he has been an ordained minister since 1955), his interest and studies in history, and his management skills gained while in charge of an extensive sales force in private industry.

As director, Don was responsible for a full-time secretary, two maintenance workers, eight student interns, and ten senior guides who worked on a volunteer basis. He coordinated the student intern program and volunteer guide staff and their training, as well as overseeing the historic properties and their upkeep, maintenance, and reconstruction. As director of a small museum, Don performed functions that would not normally fall under the director's realm in a larger organization. A typical day might also include the following tasks, which he admits were his favorites:

Conducting tours

Assisting with cooking demonstrations at the site's Summer Kitchen

Working in the gift shop or the Red Brick Store

Repairing buildings

Trimming trees, planting flowers, weeding, and cutting grass (all thirty-four acres of it)

Finding That Job

The Official Museum Directory, put out by the American Association of Museums, is a valuable resource found in the reference section of most libraries. In addition to its pages and pages of history museums and historic houses, buildings, and sites, it lists scores of historical and preservation societies, boards, agencies, councils, commissions, foundations, and research industries.

You could decide on a region where you'd like to work, then approach your choices with a phone call, resume and cover letter, or personal visit.

The American Association of Museums puts out a monthly newsletter called *Aviso*. At least half of each issue is devoted to listings for employment opportunities and internships.

Here are just a few examples of the types of jobs advertised in one issue (because these jobs are no longer open, the employers are not identified here):

HISTORIAN II   The state historical society of a northwest state is seeking a Historian II to manage the society's scholarly history magazine. Responsibilities include editing agency newsletters, developing materials for state historic sites, and providing assistance with planning the society's public programs. Minimum qualifications: M.A. in history, English, or journalism, plus proven experience in editing, design, and layout. Salary: $25,000 to $38,000.

MUSEUM ARCHIVIST   A public museum in the Midwest is seeking a half-time archivist to manage its collection of materials related to local history. Minimum requirement of bachelor's degree in archives administration, U.S. history, or library science, and three years professional experience.

DIRECTOR   Director for historic house museum and garden. Seeking creative, energetic individual to oversee exciting house museum. Responsibilities include collections management, exhibit and educational program development. Background in decorative arts and ability to work with board and volunteers important.

SITE DIRECTOR   Famous American author's home. All facets of historic site management including staffing, interpretation, and event planning. Museum management degree or equivalent, plus proven experience. Salary: middle to upper $30,000s.

INTERNSHIP   A museum of archaeology and anthropology at an eastern university anticipates funding for a nine-month collections management internship. Interns participate in a comprehensive training program and supervise volunteers in storage renovations and computer inventory of a designated collection. Candidate should be interested in a museum career and have a background in archaeology/anthropology or museum studies. Stipend: $10,000.

For More Information

The following three reports are published by the American Association of Museums. They may be ordered by contacting:

American Association of Museums
Attn: Bookstore
1575 Eye Street NW, Suite 400
Washington, DC 20005
www.aam-us.org

Careers in Museums: A Variety of Vocations. Gives a broad overview of professional career opportunities in museums, suggests educational qualifications and experience for specific positions, and provides information on how to obtain internships. It also lists job placement resources.

Museum Studies Programs: Guide to Evaluation. Answers questions about the curriculum and quality of museum studies programs.

Graduate Training in Museum Studies: What Students Need to Know. Helps future professionals assess training options in museum studies, including certification, advanced degrees, and internships.

Jobs for Structure Lovers
Preserving the Past

Architectural historians, architectural conservators, curators of structures, restoration architects, and other preservationists all share a love of historic buildings and architecture. They might specialize in a particular period or style, fascinated by Victorian gingerbread, strong red brick, or Federal woodwork and old frame farmhouses and barns. Most, however, are generalists, possessing knowledge that crosses the centuries. These professionals are good researchers or artists who have strong organizational skills and share an interest in the environment as well as history.

The activity of preservation includes several different categories that are outlined here:

Adaptive Reuse—providing a new function for older structures that would otherwise be demolished. For example, a defunct mill is converted into an office building or a college.

Architectural Conservation—using special techniques to halt further deterioration of building materials.

Restoration (often prefaced with "Historical" or "Architectural")—involving the meticulous return of a building to its former appearance at a particular period in history.

Rehabilitation or Renovation—altering or upgrading existing buildings and structures.

Architectural Conservators

Architectural conservators are not necessarily registered architects. They might have started out in the construction and contracting field, gaining along the way specialized technical experience in problems that occur with historic buildings. Some of these problems involve the historic building fabric, such as cracks in foundations and walls, water seepage, and cleaning and repair of the building. Architectural conservators understand how buildings were constructed during earlier periods and know what kinds of complications result from the natural course of time and different climatic and environmental conditions. They are familiar with building materials, roofs, windows, exterior cladding, and various reconstruction types, such as wood-frame or masonry-clad structures.

Architectural conservators are also sometimes known as curators of structures.

What It's Like to Be a Structures Curator

A curator, in the general sense of the word, is a caregiver—someone who takes care of, for example, art collections, research documents, textiles, or historic buildings. Curators of structures work in art and history museums, living history museums, and for historical societies and associations.

Mark Fortenberry was the curator of structures with the Nantucket Historical Association from 1987 to 1994. He was responsible for the maintenance of the twelve different historic sites owned and operated by the association, and he was specifically concerned with architectural accuracy in terms of period. He also supervised contractors and technicians hired to perform restorations and construct reproductions. Some of the sites included the Oldest House, the Hawden House, the Thomas Macy Warehouse, and the Old Mill. Mark talks about his former duties:

"When I first came to the association, I was involved heavily with fieldwork—replication and carpentry. As curator of structures, I worked more on an administrative level; I coordinated the restoration and repair work that goes on in the buildings. This involved meetings with architects, long-range planning, scheduling, and budgets. We continually upgraded each building as the budget permitted; we not only did routine maintenance, but we handled more serious work in terms of maintaining the historical integrity of the building and its presentation to the public. We were also concerned with safety to the public, security systems, providing handicap access, and environmental upgrading such as cooling and heating systems.

"I also worked closely with the different offices within the association. For example, we refurbished the interior of one of the house museums, so I coordinated with the curator of collections on that.

"My job was multifaceted. Because we were a relatively small organization—sixteen or so full-time professionals—I had to be prepared to take on a wide range of tasks. Normally, a better-funded organization would have an architect on staff, would have someone else in charge of security, but those duties all fell under my umbrella."

Background

Mark grew up in Nantucket, a town where every building is on the National Register of Historic Places. Under those conditions, it's easy to see how his interest in history developed. Before joining the Nantucket Historical Association as a full-time employee, Mark was self-employed as a restoration carpenter for more than twenty years. He also worked with the Massachusetts Historic Commission and did volunteer work for the Nantucket Historic Commission, designing exhibits and constructing showcases, among other things.

He has always enjoyed working on older buildings. On the island, there is a strong sensitivity toward maintaining the feeling that Nantucket is from another time. With Mark's experience and love of Nantucket, it was only natural that the Nantucket Historical Association would invite him on board as a full-time curator.

Restoration Architect

A restoration architect or an architect specializing in historic preservation has much of a general architect's experience. He or she understands how to plan spaces, how to organize construction materials, and how to put together construction documents.

The difference between a general architect and a restoration architect is that the latter's work experience has primarily been focused on historic buildings. In addition, the restoration architect will have a specialized knowledge and understanding of federal, state, and local regulations with regard to historic preservation and will also be aware of the standards set by the particular style of architecture.

What It's Like to Be a Restoration Architect

Peter Benton earned a bachelor's degree in architecture in 1972 from the University of Virginia in Charlottesville. He worked for several years for various firms in Philadelphia and Washington, D.C., then went on to complete his master's of architecture degree from the University of Pennsylvania in 1979.

He is now a senior associate with John Milner and Associates, Inc., a midsize architectural firm in West Chester, Pennsylvania, specializing in historic preservation. He joined the staff there in 1984 and has worked on a variety of projects during the past two decades. Peter talks about his profession:

"Initially, I had relatively little training in preservation, but I was exposed to the idea of ecological planning at the University of Pennsylvania. I saw the philosophical connection between an ecological approach to the landscape and to the buildings, and that led me to historic preservation. I went to work for four or five years for an ecological planning firm, and it was there my interest developed further.

"I've been responsible for all sorts of properties—anything from small, privately owned residential-scale houses from the eighteenth century to high-style nineteenth-century mansions. In addition, I've worked with historic commercial and industrial buildings from the nineteenth century, restoring them or practicing what we call adaptive reuse. For example, we recently converted an old mill into an office building and a farmhouse into a meeting facility. Another category I've worked with includes monumental buildings, such as a city hall or large federal buildings."

The Nine Steps in a Restoration Project

1. The restoration architect first meets with the client and determines what his or her goals are for the property.

2. The restoration architect does an existing conditions analysis of the site, looks at the historical development of the building over time, and takes photographs, field measurements, and written notes.

3. Next, the restoration architect does a schematic plan, making preliminary drawings and sketches, describing a design to the client for the client's approval. This stage could take four weeks or so.

4. Once the client approves the project, the restoration architect produces an outline of the scope of the work and figures an order of magnitude cost estimate.

5. After that stage is approved, the next phase is to work on design development documents. This involves the use of more detailed drawings and can take from six to eight weeks.

6. During the next eight to twelve weeks, construction documents including drawings and specifications are produced.

7. The contractor is selected during the bidding phase.

8. Construction plans are reviewed before actually beginning work.

9. The restoration architect makes frequent visits to the site while the project is in progress. Construction time varies but could take eight months or a year and a half, depending upon the scope of the project.

Salaries

Someone fresh from graduate school can expect to earn from $27,000 to $29,000 per year, depending upon the size of the firm, the importance of the project, and the region of the country. Advancement would depend upon ability and accomplishments. An experienced architect with five years or more at the project manager level could expect to earn about $40,000 a year in a midsize firm. Those with specializations in demand can earn more. Most firms offer paid internships for graduate students.

Architectural Historian

Architectural historians are historians with an interest in architecture. They are generally not registered architects. They often work with restoration architects, however, conducting specialized investigations and performing all the research necessary to get a restoration project underway. They dig up a building's history—when it was constructed, what its original purpose was, how long it was vacant, whether any changes had been made. They then put together a historic structures report for the architect who wants to make his or her restoration work as accurate as possible.

Architectural historians can work in academic settings, for private architectural firms, and for government agencies concerned with historic preservation.

The minimum requirement for an architectural historian is an undergraduate degree in history or architectural history, although most positions require a graduate degree.

Historical Interiors Designer

To achieve complete authenticity, the interior of a historic building must be given as much attention as the exterior, especially if the building will be used as a museum open to the public.

Historic interiors designers can be architects or specially trained professionals. They must be experienced in the investigation, documentation, research, and analysis of the lighting, furnishings, finishes, and decorative arts of building interiors. Historic interiors specialists generally work as part of a team with the restoration architect and conservator.

The National Trust for Historic Preservation

The National Trust for Historic Preservation is a nonprofit organization with more than 250,000 individual members. Most of the National Trust's funding comes from membership dues, corporation and foundation grants, endowment income, and merchandise sales. About 22 percent comes from a matching grant awarded by the U.S. Congress through the U.S. Department of the Interior.

The National Trust's mission is, in part, to preserve and revitalize the livability of U.S. communities by leading the nation in saving America's historic environments. It provides technical advice and financial assistance to nonprofit organizations and public agencies engaged in preservation, as well as to the general public. The National Trust also acts as an advocate for protection of the country's heritage in the courts and with legislative and regulatory agencies.

The National Trust believes that the employment outlook in the historic preservation field has grown dramatically since the early 1980s. Its concerns have enlarged from a relatively small number of historic sites, museums, and buildings to historic neighborhoods, commercial districts, and rural landscapes.

The growing sophistication of the field is reflected in the greater diversity of professionals who contribute to preservation work. Historians, curators, and other museum professionals are now joined by architects, lawyers, designers, realtors, planners, developers, mortgage lenders, and others. Once found working only in museums, libraries, and historical societies, preservationists now are also employed in real estate firms that specialize in historical properties and in financial institutions that invest in older neighborhoods.

The National Trust employs many specialists in its national office in Washington, D.C., and in its seven regional offices. In addition, the National Trust owns and operates eighteen historic house museums. It also publishes *Preservation Magazine* and *Preservation Advocate News*, which are distributed to members.

The latter lists job opportunities and internships within both the
National Trust and outside organizations. To join, contact:

National Trust for Historic Preservation
1785 Massachusetts Avenue NW
Washington, DC 20036
www.nthp.org

For More Information

You may wish to obtain the *Guide to Graduate Degree Programs
in Architectural History*, compiled by Richard Betts. It is available by contacting:

Society of Architectural Historians
1365 North Astor Street
Chicago, IL 60610
www.sah.org

Jobs in Historical Societies
Explaining the Past

T he mission of most preservation boards and historical societies is to preserve, protect, defend, and promote the cultural, social, economic, environmental, and architectural integrity of their particular district or historic site.

Preservation boards and historical societies offer full-time employment or volunteer opportunities for most of the career categories discussed in this book. Architectural historians, archivists, restoration architects, researchers, design experts, curators, information officers, and administrators work as a team to achieve their goals.

Many boards and societies are membership funded; others might receive government or private grants to carry on their work. The better-funded operations are able to hire specialists to work in their particular fields. Boards and societies with limited funds rely heavily on professionals willing to volunteer their time. The few paid employees take on a variety of tasks crossing career categories.

Information Officer

Although George Neary's official title was administrative director of the Miami Design Preservation League, he also functioned as the sole full-time information officer for the League's Art Deco District.

George earned his bachelor's degree in history at St. Anselm College in Manchester, New Hampshire, in 1970. After teaching for many years, he moved to Miami and started with the Miami Design Preservation League as a volunteer in September 1991. In March 1992, he was hired as a full-time employee. In 1999, George went on to become the director of cultural tourism with the Greater Miami Convention and Visitors Bureau.

George talks about his former job with the Miami Design Preservation League:

"It's a membership-funded organization, operating solely on membership dues, conducting tours, and putting on special events throughout the year. My assistant and I were the league's only paid employees. Everyone else was a volunteer. We had more than forty volunteers, which included a cadre of dedicated tour guides and office helpers. We also had the chairperson and the board and various committee heads and members—all volunteer professionals.

"The most important task we focused on was the preservation of the Art Deco District. Our governmental affairs committee worked with the city on zoning and other issues to protect the district from demolition or misuse. We also had an executive committee, an architectural task force, an archivist, educational committees, tour committees, special events committees, historians, and writers.

"Most of my time was spent in the role of information officer, working with the public. I made sure all members were kept informed of what was going on in the District. I handled huge mailings and sent out press releases or called the radio stations when special shows were scheduled.

"When we were putting on a major event, such as the Art Deco Weekend, I had to make sure that everything ran smoothly. I was also involved with budgeting, assigning tasks to staff members, and supervising tour guides. Occasionally I gave tours myself to special-interest groups from out of town.

"I also worked as a liaison with the city, state, and federal governments. We rallied the troops, lobbying to halt demolition permits and getting laws passed to protect the district.

"I arranged for monthly speakers and encouraged our members to attend. The members were very important to the whole operation. When they joined the league, their dues supported our activities. Members were entitled to certain privileges, such as receiving the newsletter we published, invitations to monthly gatherings and lectures, and our annual meeting, which was also open to the public."

Tour Guides and Docents

It is debatable whether there is any difference between the term *tour guide* and the most common usage of the word *docent*. Although the *Random House College Dictionary* defines *docent* as "a college or university lecturer" and *privatdocent* as "a lecturer paid directly by his or her students," many consider a docent synonymous with a tour guide.

Depending on your place of employment, a tour guide may or may not be in costume. A tour guide is not primarily responsible for conducting his or her own research and does not usually portray one particular character. In addition, a tour guide doesn't usually speak from a prepared script; a tour guide must have a broader, more general knowledge of the area and period.

Tour guides may be employed by the federal or state government, historical societies, museums, or by a private enterprise. They can also be self-employed.

Tour guides might ride in front of a bus or boat, microphone in hand; be stationed in a particular building or site, such as a church, museum, or fort; share space with visitors in a horse-drawn carriage or buggy; or lead visitors around on foot on historical walking tours.

What It's Like to Be a Tour Guide in Miami Beach's Art Deco District

Most people used to think of Miami Beach as the place everyone's grandmother lives. For a long time, Collins Avenue and Ocean Drive, packed with residential hotels and condominiums, did cater to the over-sixty set. But in the last twenty years, the demographics, as well as the topography, have been changing.

Jeff Donnelly is a volunteer tour guide for the Miami Design Preservation League. He knows the area as well as anyone. Monday through Friday he teaches history and political science at a local day school in Dade County. And for the past fourteen years on Saturday mornings, he's been donning his Panama hat and walking shoes and taking groups on ninety-minute strolling tours through Miami Beach's restored Art Deco District.

"Miami Beach is an exciting place to live these days," Jeff explains. "Young professionals, artists, models, movie production people—they're all flocking here now. We've become very chic."

After cautioning the twenty or so in his group—from New York, Texas, Colorado, and nearby Fort Lauderdale—about the strong Florida sun ("If anyone feels dehydrated, please raise your hand before you pass out"), he provides them with more than just a passing glimpse into Miami's new mystique.

"As elderly residents moved into nursing homes or passed away, investors and developers began buying up and renovating the run-down buildings," he says. "In the process, they uncovered the fantasy seaside resort that had first inspired the original boom back in the 1920s and 1930s.

"There were five major architects responsible for the district. Although they were commercial competitors, they were also coffee-klatch friends. If someone's building supplies hadn't arrived on time or if someone ran short, they lent materials back and forth. This, of course, explains the high level of style consistency throughout the district."

The old establishments, once painted white and trimmed with only powder blue, aquamarine, or the peaches and pinks of aging flamingos, have now received fresh face-lifts and glow with a contemporary pastel palette. Bands of lavender, blue, yellow, aqua, and a whole spectrum of pinks whimsically decorate ocean-front hotels, sidewalk cafés, model agencies, and apartment buildings.

Miami Beach can boast one of the largest concentrations of art deco buildings in the country: more than eight hundred structures contribute to the historic or architectural nature of the city's Art Deco District. The result is a Disneyesque urban streetscape, as fanciful as Victorian gingerbread, with the promise of campy humor and fun.

"You'd almost expect to see flappers strolling arm in arm or Al Capone roaring up in his jalopy," observed one member of the tour group. In fact, it's rumored that Al Capone often ate at the Park Central, one of the hotels along Ocean Drive, with his bodyguards perched on the overhead balcony for protection. Whether that story is true or not, the gangster movie *Scarface* was filmed there.

The term *art deco*, meaning a bold and linear form of art combining art moderne, cubism, futurism, and expressionism, wasn't coined until the 1960s, but it refers to the style that became popular in the 1920s and 1930s, originating in Paris. In its day, Miami Beach's architecture was considered ultramodern; the goal was to be futuristic, to look ahead. In the grip of the Great Depression, the architects and designers wanted to convey the message that happy days were coming.

But the art deco area is not a historic district that seeks to preserve exactly what was there in the twenties and thirties.

"We're not a Williamsburg," says Jeff. "Our philosophy is what we call 'adaptive reuse'—restoration projects focus on designs with contemporary uses. It allows for a larger variety of colors and for more of the surface areas to be given over to color."

Anyone who wants to renovate must bring their plans to the Miami Preservation League Review Board for approval. "The Tuesday night meetings are a great source of local entertainment," says Jeff. "The number of arguments presented over color choices are fascinating."

The Miami Design Preservation League was established in 1976 and is the oldest art deco organization in the world. For three years, the league cataloged the art deco and Mediterranean revival–style buildings, earning a listing in the National Register of Historic Places. The league's main function now is to guard against demolitions, incompatible construction, and false restorations.

"We don't want new construction to completely imitate the old style," Donnelly says. "There's a Kentucky Fried Chicken that slipped by before the review board was established. It looks so much like a building from the twenties—it confuses people."

But the hotels that line Ocean Drive are the real thing. Many are named after posh New York establishments to convey a sense of luxury—the Ritz, the Waldorf Towers; some are named after the designers' family members—the Victor, the Adrian.

It's not only the bright colors that attract the eye. Special attention to form, detail, and vertical and horizontal lines makes up the art deco style. Buildings have varying themes: streamline rounded corners accented with "eyebrows," needlelike finials pointing skyward (the Breakwater Hotel's allegedly were used in an early Buck Rogers film), rare etched-glass windows, fluted cornices, stepped rooflines, horizontal racing stripes, and nautical moderne porthole windows.

The Avalon hotel has added a special touch to complete the pretty picture—a 1950 yellow-and-white Oldsmobile rimmed with shiny chrome is regularly parked in front of the yellow building. Quite a number of advertising and modeling agencies use the hotel for a backdrop on photographic shoots.

Indeed, any morning of the week, when the early eastern light splashes across the soft colors, five or six different shoots are usually in progress. Scenes from the TV show "Miami Vice" were frequently shot along Ocean Drive, and more and more celebrities visit the area.

Regular special events add even more life to this spirited district. One of those events is the Art Deco Weekend, held annually on the second weekend of January. It relives the days of the Big Band, speakeasies, and street theater against Miami Beach's classic art deco backdrop. Antique cars, period artwork, collectibles, and memorabilia carry visitors back to the Roaring Twenties.

Nighttime brings a new dimension to the Art Deco District. Neon tube lighting was first invented in the late 1930s, and Ocean Drive was a showcase for this exciting new discovery.

"It must have been a magical experience for those seeing the glowing, colorful lights against the glass block for the first time," says Jeff.

Many of the lobbies inside the hotels are equally magical. Original murals and paintings of the era decorate the walls, and colorful terrazzo stone chips cover the floors in geometric patterns.

Jeff points out the last stop, the Blackstone Hotel, where George Gershwin reputedly wrote "Porgy and Bess," then steers his group back to the Art Deco Welcome Center.

"It's ironic, really," Jeff concludes. "We've put a lot of effort into preserving an era that actually stood for forward movement, growth, and development. But the architects of the time hit on just the right note for Miami Beach. What was beautiful then is even more beautiful now. It's certainly worth preserving."

For more information on the Art Deco District, contact:

Miami Design Preservation League
P.O. Box 190180
Miami Beach, FL 33119
www.mdpl.org

What It's Like to Be a Docent for the Nantucket Historical Association

Jeremy Slavitz was a paid docent for the Nantucket Historical Association. Although he grew up in a location noted for its historical significance, it wasn't until he attended college that his interest in history developed. He wasn't sure what he wanted to do, so he enrolled in a variety of classes. The history courses interested him the most, and he discovered it was important to work in a discipline he enjoyed. He graduated from the University of Massachusetts, Amherst, in 1992 with a bachelor's degree in history, specializing in naval history. The summer of 1992 was his first season as a docent. He later picked up additional responsibilities over the years. He became docent trainer, worked with the educational programs for children, and is now coordinator of public programs. Jeremy talks about his former job:

"What I liked most about working as a docent for the Historical Association was that it gave me a chance to work in history, but I wasn't stuck in a closet doing research. I could get out and talk to people. I gave information every day, struggling to make it interesting for people. I enjoyed the challenge.

"The docents always work in pairs, and that's one of the other aspects that helped to make the job fun. There were several other college students employed as well as the older residents. We alternated taking guests through. On a rainy day, we were very busy, with not much time to rest. When the sun was out, most visitors to Nantucket headed for the beach. Then the day at the association went a bit slower.

"The docents with the Historical Association try to portray our museums throughout their history. Rather than just identifying a certain object, a chair or a table, we tried to give visitors a more three-dimensional picture of the people who were living there through various time periods, as well as the different ways the building was used.

"For example, one of the properties I worked in is Nantucket's Oldest House. It was built in 1686 by Jethro Coffin. He was a wealthy businessman, and at that time his house was one of the largest on the island and was considered the most prestigious. We showed the house as it was then, and we showed it as it was during the eighteenth century after another owner, Nathaniel Paddock, bought it. He was a weaver, and he worked on his loom in the home. During his time, as the island population grew, the house was considered to be of modest proportions and no longer held the same prestige. We also showed the house as it is now, a small structure with three rooms on the ground floor and two rooms upstairs.

"I didn't work from a prepared script. There is a general guideline to follow, but I had the freedom to tailor my presentation based on who was visiting. One summer, there was a local boy whose parents were members of the historical association. They gave him their pass, which allows admission to about twelve different properties, put him on his bicycle, and sent him on his way. He would bring his friends, and over the course of the summer, he followed me around to the different sites where I worked. He'd wait until most of the other visitors had left, so I could show him parts of the buildings he would find the most interesting. They peered up chimneys and climbed through root cellars and figured out how the loom worked. They had a great time. Someone else would have an entirely different interest, so I would focus on another aspect for them."

How Nantucket Historical Association Docents Are Trained

"The training process was very enjoyable. In each museum there is a book that has been put together that includes all the known information about the house or building. On top of that, there are people here who have done this for years, so a lot of the training has to do with oral history. New docents are learning from people who have learned from people before them. Some of the older docents have lived on the island all of their lives, and they can pass down the history, as well as their own experiences with the property."

Hours and Salary

Jeremy put in as many hours as possible as a docent and generally worked a forty-hour week spread over six days. Because one of the museums is open at night, he was also on duty for some evening hours.

He was paid $6 an hour when he worked as a docent, but docents are currently paid $11 per hour.

Further Reading

Confessions of a Tour Leader, by Baxter and Corinne Geeting (Prima Publishing), offers a witty and sophisticated look at the real-life experiences of a college faculty couple who became summertime tour leaders.

Jobs for Diggers
Uncovering the Past

M ost history professionals are diggers, both literally and figuratively—they dig up information from the past. Some dig through mounds of dirt for relics and other evidence of past civilizations and cultures; others seek facts digging through mounds of paper.

Archaeologist

Archaeology is one subdivision of the field of anthropology. Archaeologists study the artifacts of past cultures to learn about their histories, customs, and living habits. They survey and excavate archaeological sites, recording and cataloging their finds. By careful analysis, archaeologists reconstruct earlier cultures and determine their influences on the present.

Archaeological sites are the physical remains of past civilizations. They can include building debris and the items found inside, in addition to trash and garbage. Usually these sites have been buried by other, later human activity or by various natural processes.

Excavation of these sites is a painstaking process conducted by professionals using modern techniques. Because these sites are so fragile, the very nature of excavating destroys some information.

With this in mind, archaeologists are careful to dig only as much as is needed to answer important questions. Frequently, archaeologists concentrate their work on sites slated for destruction to make room for new highway or building construction.

Archaeologists work in a variety of settings. The following chart lists these settings and the duties specific to each.

Setting	Duties	Working Conditions
Universities and Colleges, Private Institutions	Teaching, Fieldwork, Research, Directing Student Fieldwork	Classroom, Labs, Office Space
Museums	Fieldwork, Research, Classifying, Preserving, Displaying	Display and Research Areas, Office Space
Public Sector (local, state, and federal government agencies)	Excavating, Surveying, Analyzing, Preserving, Recording Remains	On-Site, Labs, Research Facilities
Private Sector (construction companies, architectural firms)	Excavating, Surveying, Preserving, Recording Remains	On-Site, Labs, Research Facilities

Archaeologists conducting fieldwork often work with several other professionals in a team effort. They are assisted by geologists, ethnologists, educators, anthropologists, ecologists, and aerial photographers.

In the field, archaeologists use a variety of tools in an excavation. These include picks, shovels, trowels, wheelbarrows, sifting boxes, pressure sprayers, and brushes. Archaeologists also make drawings and sketches on-site and take notes and photographs.

What It Takes to Become an Archaeologist

Do you have what it takes to become an archaeologist? Take this self-evaluation quiz and find out. Answer "yes" or "no" to each of the following questions.

1. I have above-average academic ability.

2. I have an avid interest in science and history.

3. Hours of strenuous activity (lifting, carrying, shoveling) do not pose a problem for me.

4. I have been told I have leadership qualities.

5. The idea of continuing study throughout my career appeals to me.

6. I am a logical and analytical thinker.

7. I enjoy working independently.

8. I function well as part of a team.

9. I believe professional ethics should be strictly adhered to.

10. I can live under primitive conditions in remote areas.

To consider yourself a potential archaeologist, you must have been able to answer "yes" for every question. Even with just one negative answer, you might want to reconsider your choice of field. Archaeology is an extremely rigorous and competitive profession.

Education

To qualify as a professional archaeologist, graduate study leading to a master's degree is necessary. A doctoral degree is often preferable. Most graduate programs in archaeology are found in anthropology departments. There are about thirty universities maintaining schools of archaeology; these are listed in the *Peterson's Guide to Graduate and Professional Programs*. To gain the necessary background at the undergraduate level, pursue a study of anthropology, history, art, geology, or a related field. At the graduate level, students following a course in archaeology would also have to include cultural and physical anthropology and linguistics in the curriculum.

Job Opportunities

Relatively few openings exist in the field of teaching archaeology. Recently, however, more federal grants and contracts have been made available for archaeological fieldwork and research. A lot of this work is being conducted in the western and southwestern states, such as Colorado, Arizona, and New Mexico. Particularly in northwestern New Mexico, there is a strong industry developing resources such as gas and oil. Because much of the land there is owned by the federal Bureau of Land Management, professional archaeologists must be hired to clear the site before gas lines or wells can be put in.

In addition to that, the building of a reservoir on the Dolores River in Colorado uncovered hundreds of archaeological sites, necessitating a great deal of archaeological work. The project, which is the largest on the continent and has a very attractive budget, has since brought many archaeologists to that area.

Interested history buffs who do not desire full-time professional careers as archaeologists, but would like to experience archaeological work, can find many opportunities to try their hands at a dig. If you are willing to invest your time—and in some cases, your money—you can easily find professionally supervised archaeological investigations taking on volunteers. These are listed in *Archaeology* magazine or in the books mentioned at the end of this section. A few other examples of places to contact are provided here:

Crow Canyon Archaeological Center
23390 County Road K
Cortez, CO 81321
www.crowcanyon.org

Earthwatch Institute
3 Clock Tower Place, Suite 100
Box 75
Maynard, MA 01754
www.earthwatch.org

Center for American Archeology
P.O. Box 366
Kampsville, IL 62053
www.caa-archeology.org

Close-Up: Crow Canyon Archaeological Center

Crow Canyon is a nonprofit research and educational institution funded by tuition fees, donations, and federal grants. It features an eighty-acre campus in southwestern Colorado, near Mesa Verde National Park, with a staff of about fifty archaeologists, educators, and support staff. In addition to its own research, the institution instructs participants, both adults and children, who want to learn about archaeology. From junior high age on, participants are taken into the field and taught excavation, recording, and documentation techniques. They also work in the lab a few days a week learning analysis techniques and methods for cleaning artifacts.

Children too young to work in the field can still participate in a simulated dig in a lab Crow Canyon has set up for that purpose. There they can learn the same excavating techniques as they sift through large, shallow sandboxes where artifacts and walls and other features are buried, just as they would be in the field.

Participants come from all over the United States on educational vacations and stay for a three-to-five-day program. Crow Canyon also works with about a dozen graduate students of archaeology a year, providing rewarding internships.

During the summer months, participants sleep in cabin tents or hogans, circular Navaho-style structures.

In Montezuma County, where Crow Canyon is located, there are more than one hundred thousand archaeological sites. Crow Canyon professionals work at two different nearby sites—Sand Canyon Pueblo and Castle Rock Pueblo, both on Bureau of Land Management land. The sites were once Anasazi Indian villages. The Anasazi are the ancestors of present-day Pueblo Indians and were in this area of Colorado from the sixth century until about the year 1300. When they vacated the area, they headed for various points south and relocated. The Crow Canyon team's research is focusing on when exactly the Anasazi left and why. They are also investigating the political and social systems of the Anasazi.

What It's Like to Be a Field Anthropologist at Crow Canyon

Kristin Kuckelman is a field anthropologist at Crow Canyon Archaeological Center. Her interest began when she was a child. Kristin's father was in the U.S. Air Force, and she traveled with her parents around the world. They were interested in different cultures and in archaeology as well and passed those interests on to their daughter. When it came time to go to college, Kristin was naturally drawn to the anthropology program. Kristin talks about her job:

"I love the variety of it. I enjoy working outdoors; I enjoy writing. And with any kind of research, there's the excitement of discovery. You're trying to solve problems, you're trying to find things out, you're trying to learn something new. And, basically, every time you go in the field, you hope you're going to learn something about a culture that no one knew before. You don't know what that's going to be; you never really know how it's going to turn out or what you're going to find.

"The sites in this particular area are very easy to discern. They have many hundreds of masonry rooms with, even after centuries, telltale piles of rubble and thousands of artifacts scattered about the ground. Just from walking around the modern ground surface, you can see the tops of the walls and the depressions in the ground indicating the subterranean chambers.

"Sand Canyon covers about four acres. Castle Rock is smaller, close to three acres, and is situated around the base of a butte, a small flat-topped mountain.

"Because of the subterranean chambers, we sometimes have to dig down to two and a half to three meters to find the actual floor of the structure. The surface rooms are shallower, but we can still have a meter, a meter and a half filled in.

"We've found lithic artifacts, which are artifacts made out of stone, such as spear and arrow points, and sandstone tools for grinding grain. We've also found tens of thousands of pottery fragments—very rarely do we find a piece that is still intact. And very rarely do we engage in refitting, trying to piece the shards together. With so many pieces scattered over the ground, it would take many years, be very, very expensive, and would certainly drive someone crazy!

"Beginning with the first week in May, which is the start of our field season, my partner and I head out to the site, set up equipment, and make sure we have the areas we want excavated all laid out and prepared. We take care of all our paperwork and any mapping we have to do so we're ready for participants to begin digging.

"During the digging season, we take participants out two or three days a week, but the first full day is spent on campus. Our educators give them a full orientation about archaeology in general. Out in the field, we give them a site tour to give them a background on what it is we're going to be digging, why we're digging, what we're trying to learn. We then give them tools and individual instruction and place them, either individually or in pairs, at the particular places we want excavated.

"Basically, we move dirt and put it in a bucket and then take it to a screening station, which is a quarter-inch mesh screen. The dirt gets sifted through the screen to make sure we're not losing any artifacts. Everybody has a different bag to keep artifacts from each excavation area separate.

"Near the end of the season, we have quite a bit of documentation and mapping to do, and we wash and analyze the artifacts. When we're finished with them, most of the artifacts are put in storage, though a few are rotated as exhibits at the Anasazi Heritage Center, a federally run curatorial facility.

"Then we have to fill the areas we've dug back in with all the screened dirt and rocks we originally dug out. The idea is if you were to walk across the site a year later, you'd never know there had been an excavation there. For safety reasons, we can't leave gaping holes in the land, and in terms of conservation, to leave a pit open to the elements would damage the site.

"Before we close it back up, we line the pit with landscaping fabric to protect it and to provide a clue in case future archaeologists are digging there but do not have access to our notes and maps. The lining would show them the site had already been excavated. There are so many sites, and to keep a site open and developed for public exhibit, as has been done at Mesa Verde, would be extremely expensive. It would also be very hard on the architecture itself. Constant maintenance would have to be performed or everything would eventually deteriorate.

"During the winter, we write up in report form everything we learned the previous summer. We also write articles for professional journals and present papers at archaeological conferences across the country."

Background
Kristin graduated in 1975 with a bachelor's degree in anthropology and psychology from Colorado Women's College (which has now merged with the University of Denver). She earned her master's degree in anthropology with a concentration in archaeology from the University of Texas at Austin in 1977.

Further Reading

Periodicals
Archaeological Fieldwork Opportunities Bulletin, compiled by the Archaeological Institute of America. It can be ordered through Kendall Hunt Publishing Company, 4050 Westmark Drive, Dubuque, IA 52001. It is a comprehensive guide to excavations, field schools, and special programs throughout the world with openings for volunteers, students, staff, and technicians.

Summer Field School List, American Anthropological Association, 4350 North Fairfax Drive, Arlington, VA 22203.

LEAP: Listing of Education in Archaeological Programs, available from LEAP coordinator, DCA/ADD, National Park Service, P.O. Box 37127, Washington, DC 20013.

Books
Archaeology: A Brief Introduction, by Brian M. Fagan
   (Prentice Hall).

Archaeology: Theories, Methods, and Practice, by Colin
   Renfrew and Paul Bahn (Thames and Hudson, New York).

Magazines
Archaeology (published by the Archaeological Institute of
   America)

National Geographic

Scientific American

Smithsonian

Professional Journals
These journals, though not available in every local library, can be
found in university libraries or in large public libraries.

American Antiquity

Historical Archaeology

Journal of Anthropological Archaeology

Journal of Field Archaeology

North American Archaeologist

Archivist

Nobody knows the exact number, but it's estimated that there are close to five thousand archives in the United States. Each of the fifty states maintains government archives, as do most city and county governments. In addition, archives can be found in universities, historical societies, museums, libraries, and private businesses.

On the national level, there is the National Archives in Washington, D.C., which looks after the records of the federal government. The Library of Congress provides information services to the U.S. Congress and technical services to all the libraries across the country.

Although archives are similar to libraries, there are distinct differences between the two. Libraries typically house materials that are published and were created with the express purpose of broad dissemination. Archives typically hold materials that were created in the course of carrying out some sort of business or activity but were never intended originally for public dissemination. For example, in an archive you might find letters from a Civil War soldier to his family. He wrote about his experiences and feelings and to let his loved ones know that he was still alive, surviving this or that battle. He never would have imagined that his correspondence would be saved for public viewing. This gives his letters credibility, an integrity as a historical source. The newspaper reporter covering the same battles is writing with a specific point of view for widespread publication, ultimately with the intention of selling newspapers.

Archives handle collections that chart the course of daily life for individuals and businesses. Some archives specifically look after materials created by their own institutions. Coca-Cola Company, for example, set up an archive years ago to have a history of what the company business was and how it prospered. New companies set up archives to keep documented records.

Other institutions, such as universities or museums, create archives that relate to their special research interests.

The material found in archives can be letters, personal papers, organizational records, and other documents. Archives created within the past one hundred years or so could also contain visual records such as photographs, postcards, prints, drawings, and sketches. Today, archives also collect tape recordings, phonograph records, movie films, videotapes, and computer-stored information.

Because archives hold firsthand information, they are valuable to anyone with an interest in the people, places, and events of the past. This group includes genealogists, museum researchers, scholars, students, writers, and historians.

As with libraries and archives, there are distinct differences between librarians and archivists in the way they operate and the methods and techniques they use to handle material. The biggest single difference is that librarians look at materials they get on an item-by-item basis. Each book is a distinct entity evaluated separately from the other books. In an archive, a single letter would usually be part of a larger collection of letters. Archivists are interested in these as a group, because one letter would only be a fragment. To really understand something about the past, the information needs to be synthesized and put together to form a collection.

Archivists provide a service to society by identifying and preserving materials with lasting value for the future. When archivists talk about their work, they discuss certain basic functions that are common to all archives. The numbers to the right of the following five areas designate the percentage of time usually spent on each duty.

1. Identification and acquisition of materials   10%

2. Arrangement and description of collections   60%

3. Preservation of collections   10%

4. Reference services   15%

5. Community outreach and public affairs   5%

What It's Like to Be the Chief Archivist at the Museum of American History

John Fleckner came to the Smithsonian in 1982 with more than a decade's experience working as an archivist for the State Historical Society of Wisconsin. He is a past president of the Society of American Archivists and has acted as a consultant on many important archives projects, including the United Negro College Fund, the Vietnam History and Archives Project, and the Native American Archives Project.

John did his undergraduate work at Colgate, in Hamilton, New York, graduating in 1963 with a bachelor's degree, with honors, in history. He earned his master's degree in American history at the University of Wisconsin in 1965. He has also amassed significant work toward a doctorate.

The archives John is responsible for acquires collections from the outside and does not handle the records generated by the museum. Its collections cover a wide range of subjects and are particularly strong in the areas of American music, advertising, and the history of technology.

At the Smithsonian, John oversees a professional staff of twelve archivists, three student interns, and close to twenty volunteers. He divides his time as follows:

1. Identification and acquisition of materials   15%

2. Supervision   50%

3. Reference services   10%

4. Administration, meetings, budget, personnel   15%

5. Outreach and public affairs   10%

John talks about how he became an archivist:

"After too many years of graduate school, pursuing a vague notion of teaching college-level history, I realized that I really didn't want to teach. I was so naive, it took a university career counselor to recognize that my history background might be anything other than an economic liability. Leaning back in her chair, she pointed out her office window to the State Historical Society of Wisconsin just across the street, and she directed me to a recently established graduate program in archives administration. The instructor would make no promises about the prospects for a job, but with a sly smile he offered that all his previous students were working. I didn't need a weatherman—as they said in those days, the early 1970s—to tell me which way the wind was blowing.

"So, it was an accident in good guidance that got me in the door. But it was the experience of doing archival work—beginning with the simplest class exercises and then a formal internship—that sealed it for me. I loved the combination of handicraft and analytical work, and I loved the intense, intimate contact with the 'stuff' of history. Before I completed my internship, I knew I wanted to be an archivist.

"Previously, as a graduate student, of course I had done some research in archives—at the Library of Congress, the College of William and Mary, and especially the State Historical Society. But the archivists had taken all the fun out of it. The materials were antiseptically put in folders, boxed, and listed. Wheeled out on carts, they were like cadavers to be dissected by first-year medical students. On occasion I even donned white gloves. The documents always seemed lifeless.

"Later, as a would-be archivist, they thrilled me. I was in charge; I would evaluate their significance, determine their order, describe their contents, and physically prepare them for their permanent resting places.

"Still, it was not so much this heady feeling of control that awed me but more the mystery, the possibilities of the records themselves. My judgments would be critical to building paths to the records for generations of researchers, across the entire spectrum of topics, and into unknown future time.

"The archival enterprise held another attractive feature for me. For all the opportunity to reconstruct the past captured in these documents, and to imagine the future research they might support, I had a well-defined task to accomplish, a product to produce, techniques and methods for proceeding, and standards against which my work would be judged. There was rigor and discipline; this was real work. And, as good fortune would have it, I soon was getting paid to do it."

Education

People get into the archives profession in a variety of traditional and unusual ways. Often in a small town, an archive is a closet in the back room of a local historical society's office. Someone volunteers to put it all together, perhaps the oldest person in the community with a strong interest in the area's history.

The standard way to become an archivist is to have an undergraduate degree with a history background and a graduate degree at least at the master's level that would involve specific course work in archives. There are thirty to fifty programs (the Society of American Archivists publishes a directory of these educational programs) that are often in graduate library schools.

Many archivists have master of library science (M.L.S.) degrees with a concentration in archives, but sometimes archives courses are taught in history departments.

Earnings

Archivists with master's degrees can expect to start out with annual salaries in the $30,000 range. Someone with ten years of experience working as an archivist with administrative responsibilities for the Smithsonian might earn $60,000 a year or more.

Genealogist

The study of genealogy, tracing family histories, has recently become one of the most popular hobbies in the United States. Many genealogy hobbyists take this interest one step beyond tracing their own family histories and become self-employed genealogists, helping others to dig up their family trees. Genealogists also are employed in historical societies and libraries with special genealogy rooms.

The Church of Jesus Christ of Latter-Day Saints in Salt Lake City, for example, has a huge repository of family information in a subterranean library. The Mormons employ genealogists all over the world, and they include genealogists who have been accredited through their own program on a list of freelance researchers. For more information, contact:

Accreditation Program
Family History Library
35 North West Temple Street
Salt Lake City, UT 84150
www.familysearch.org

Other genealogists find work teaching their skills to others in adult education classes, by editing genealogy magazines, or by writing books or newspaper genealogy columns.

Most genealogists are not formally trained, though specializing in genealogy is possible through some university history and library science programs. In addition, a genealogist can become board certified. For information on certification requirements and procedures, write to:

Board for Certification of Genealogists
P.O. Box 5816
Falmouth, VA 22403

Earnings

Salaries vary depending upon the institution where a genealogist is employed and upon the level of expertise he or she has reached. Self-employed genealogists make anywhere from $15 to $35 an hour or more.

Getting Started

The National Genealogy Society makes the following suggestions for beginners:

QUESTION OLDER FAMILY MEMBERS.   Encourage them to talk about their childhoods and relatives and listen carefully for clues they might inadvertently drop. Learn good interviewing techniques so you ask questions that elicit the most productive answers. Use a tape recorder and try to verify each fact through a separate source.

VISIT YOUR LOCAL LIBRARY.   Become familiar with historical and genealogical publications (a few sources are provided at the end of this chapter and in Appendix D) and contact local historical societies and the state library and archives in your state capital. Seek out any specialty ethnic or religious libraries and visit cemeteries.

VISIT COURTHOUSES.   Cultivate friendships with busy court clerks. Ask to see source records such as wills, deeds, marriage books, and birth and death certificates.

ENTER INTO CORRESPONDENCE.   Write to other individuals or societies involved with the same families or regions. Contact foreign embassies in Washington, D.C. Restrict yourself to asking only one question in each letter you send. Include the information you have already uncovered. Include a self-addressed, stamped envelope to encourage replies.

BECOME COMPUTER LITERATE.   Members of the National
Genealogical Society can participate in a special computer interest section. It encourages the use of computers in research,
record management, and data sharing.

KEEP PAINSTAKING RECORDS.   Use printed family group
sheets or pedigree charts. Develop a well-organized filing system
so you'll be able to easily find your information. Keep separate
records for each family you research.

WRITE TO THE NATIONAL GENEALOGICAL SOCIETY.   Take
advantage of its forty-six-page book—*Beginners in Genealogy*—
its charts, and its library loan program. You can also enroll in a
home-study course called American Genealogy: A Basic Course.

Writing and Photography
Documenting the Past

M any innovative people have combined a love of history with other talents or acquired skills. With a good imagination and a lot of drive and persistence, a dedicated history buff can bring in extra income or create a specialized career.

Here are a few successful ventures that might spark some ideas of your own.

Writing

What It's Like to Be a Desktop Publisher

Prudy Taylor Board, a published author, creative writing instructor, and staff writer for her local newspaper, has established a sideline called Prudy's Press. She researches and self-publishes pamphlets covering the historic sites in her hometown of Fort Myers on the west coast of Florida. Some of her topics include Sanibel Island's famous lighthouse; the Burroughs Home, which is on the National Register of Historic Places; and an account of the history of Fort Myers. Prudy talks about her enterprises:

"I attended a national convention for writers in San Antonio, and while I was there, I paid a visit to the Alamo. There was a little booklet on sale for $1.95, a short write-up of the fort's history. I knew from all my years in Fort Myers that there was no inexpensive tourist information available there. I had a file cabinet full of information at home, and I realized I could do the same for attractions in my own area. And that's how Prudy's Press was born.

"Being an active member of both the Southwest Florida Historical Society and the Fort Myers Historical Museum has helped me when it comes time to do my research. The two organizations have opened their archives to me. I also talk to the old-timers in the neighborhood and regularly visit the public library, where all the past issues of newspapers dating back to 1894 are on microfilm.

"When I start a book project, I run a little ad in the paper asking for information, or I generate a press release announcing the new book. I ask people to share their memories and photographs with me.

"After I'm finished writing, I do the layout on my computer using a desktop publishing package. Then I take the camera-ready copy to my local printer and pay him for the printing, paper, folding, collating, and stapling. My cost runs between fifty and seventy-five cents per copy.

"I sell the booklets at a wholesale price of $1.50 per copy to bookstores, museums, and other tourist attraction gift shops. Or, I acquire a mailing list of selected markets and send out samples. I generally sell between fifty and a hundred booklets a month.

"I've also been contacted by various organizations to write pamphlets and booklets for them on topics of their own choosing, for which I am paid a set rate. And, in addition to a booklet and map I put together for a historic walking tour enterprise, I've coauthored three full-length books published by Donning: *A Pictorial History of Lee County*, *Pages from the Past*, and *Historic Fort Myers*."

Prudy also gives talks on local history to different civic organizations and clubs and acts as a tour guide for an occasional historic cruise or bus tour. Her fee ranges from free, with the opportunity to sell her booklets, to $200.

What It's Like to Be a Newspaper Columnist

Cookie O'Brien, a longtime resident of St. Augustine, Florida, and information officer for the city's preservation board, has also started a sideline. She writes a frequent column for her local newspaper, delving into the private lives of historic figures from her region. In true soap-opera fashion, which fascinates her readers, she reports the loves and scandals, adventures and tragedies that surrounded early St. Augustine inhabitants.

How to Get Started

Writers can duplicate both Prudy's and Cookie's efforts, disseminating local historic tidbits and covering characters and events from their own regions. After a trip to the public library, try writing a few sample booklets or columns, then approach museum gift shops, bookstores, civic groups, or your local editor with a query letter, phone call, or visit.

Writing Historical Novels

On a larger scale, requiring higher degrees of skill and perseverance, writers have been entertaining readers throughout the years with epic forays into fictionalized history.

Imaginary characters are interwoven with real events and places; romance, pathos, and mystery often play a large part in the action. The author's research skills and attention to authentic detail (among other things) are what can make or break a potential sale to a publisher. Our hero can't be posing for photographs before the camera was invented or wearing a style of clothing that didn't come into fashion for fifty years. Some successful authors in the genre are Norah Lofts and Victoria Holt.

Writing Coffee-Table Books

Coffee-table books are so named because they are handsomely designed volumes intended to be kept on display, rather than tucked away on a bookshelf. They usually focus on a particular topic and are illustrated by beautiful photographs. History is a common source for subject matter, from the events of the past to the objects, structures, and cultures left behind.

Close-Up: Painted Ladies

Michael Larsen and Elizabeth Pomada, successful literary agents and authors, moved from New York and set up shop in San Francisco in the early 1970s. While their agency was still in its infancy, Michael took a part-time job as a taxi driver—and got a chance to explore their adopted city in depth. In the process, he discovered a rich treasure of American craft work: fanciful Victorian houses. His reaction was typical of any savvy literary agent and history lover.

"Seeing those glorious houses bathed in golden California light—I knew there had to be a book in it," Michael explains.

So far, there have been six books in it. The series documents Victorians in San Francisco and across the country.

The term *painted lady*, now used generically to describe a multicolored Victorian home, was coined by Michael and Elizabeth in their first book, *Painted Ladies: San Francisco's Resplendent Victorians*. The phrase has gone a long way toward saving Victorian homes from the wrecking ball.

"Houses of historic value, often in neighborhoods that had seen better days, were being torn down all across America,"

Elizabeth explains. "Someone needed to call attention to the problem—to tell people that these homes often qualified for federal loans and that they could be given a face-lift with a new coat of paint."

The use of contrasting colors brings out the ruffles, flourishes, and other fairy-tale features common to Victorian homes but that have been hidden under years of neglect and layers of white paint. Typical Victorian colors encompass a polychrome rainbow and include raspberry, plum, rose, grape, clay pink, pewter, lime green, and gold.

The authors write in their introduction, "Because of their beauty, craftsmanship, inexhaustible variety, the quality of materials that went into them, and their sheer numbers, Victorians are the greatest gift of America's architectural heritage."

Painted Ladies: San Francisco's Resplendent Victorians sparked what is now thought of as a color revolution. Since 1978, when the book was published, this colorist movement has spread from San Francisco to cities throughout the country.

The book has become the mainstay for the network of Victorian home owners, preservationists, historians, architects, craftspeople, city planners, and magazine publishers. It also prompted a surge in revitalizing Victorian homes throughout America. The second book of the series, *Daughters of Painted Ladies*, covers this new generation of painted ladies in six regions. It instructs home owners how to create their own painted ladies, offers suggestions for saving derelict Victorian structures, and lists valuable resources such as national preservation organizations, books, magazines, color consultants, and suppliers.

The sixth in the series, *America's Painted Ladies*, is a tribute to history, color, and architecture. The duo have also coauthored another book; this one is about Artistic License, a San Francisco Bay area guild that is revitalizing Victorian crafts.

Both Michael Larsen and Elizabeth Pomada are extremely proud of their roles in preserving an important facet of America's architectural heritage.

Photography

Many writers team up with photographers, as Michael Larsen and Elizabeth Pomada did for several of their Painted Ladies books. But a photographer with writing and/or marketing skills—and a focused project—can set out on his or her own to capture America's heritage.

In addition to colorful Victorian houses, the intricate iron balconies in New Orleans's French Quarter and the stately doors and town houses of historic Boston have all been preserved by cameras. The resulting photographs have been reproduced as postcards, posters, greeting cards, calendars, and coffee-table books.

Here are a few other suggestions. By exploring in your own neighborhood or traveling through the country, you can add to the list.

Historic forts

Early trains

Old sailing vessels

Vintage clothing and costumes

Civil War battle sites

Art deco architecture and neon displays

Living history museums

Antique collections and collectibles

Shaker furniture

Victorian crafts

Photography is also an essential element of many history-related fields. Photographers are often employed by archaeologists, restoration architects, and museum collection managers. The photographic possibilities are endless, limited only by your imagination.

How to Market Your Work

Photographers with darkroom facilities or access to a good lab can have their own postcards, posters, and calendars printed and duplicated for minimal costs. Approaching bookstores and gift shops in the region your work covers can result in consignment arrangements or outright sales.

Distributors become necessary for projects with more national appeal. *The Literary Marketplace*, a volume readily available at any library, lists the different distributors and the products they handle.

Greeting card companies are always on the lookout for interesting art. *Photographer's Market* and *Writer's Market* are annual directories that list galleries, publishers, greeting card and calendar producers, and other potential markets for your work. These books also contain articles that explain how to approach these markets.

Proposing a Coffee-Table Book

A coffee-table book with color photographs is a much more expensive undertaking—and definitely outside the personal budget of most photographers and writers. Proposing your idea to a publisher is the only way to go.

Michael Larsen, in addition to his Painted Ladies series, is the author of the definitive book on the subject of book proposals. Appropriately titled *How to Write a Book Proposal*, it covers everything you need to know to create a successful proposal, including nine criteria for judging your idea, eight things editors look for, and how to submit illustrations. The guide is published by Writer's Digest Books. However, even with the most carefully crafted proposal, you most likely will run into resistance. Many publishers shy away from such projects because of the cost involved.

Michael Larsen and Elizabeth Pomada, even as established literary agents, had difficulty at first convincing a publisher to take on their Painted Ladies project. Some were put off because of the cost; others felt that their first book, which covered only San Francisco, was too regional in scope and wouldn't sell enough copies to make it profitable. They were wrong.

An editor from Dutton made a trip to San Francisco and was immediately captivated by the idea. Six books later, and with hundreds of thousands of copies in print, the Painted Ladies series continues the movement in Victorian restoration.

If your idea is solid, the quality of your work is exceptional, and you don't give up easily (it took Michael and Elizabeth a year and a half to find their enthusiastic editor), approaching a publisher can eventually pay off.

For More Information

Further Reading

America's Painted Ladies: The Ultimate Celebration of Our Victorians, by Elizabeth Pomada and Michael Larsen. Photographs by Douglas Keister (Dutton-Studio Books).

Historic Preservation Through Victorian Crafts: A Portrait of Artistic License, by Michael Larsen and Elizabeth Pomada (Dutton-Studio Books).

How to Write a Book Proposal, by Michael Larsen (Writer's Digest Books).

The Literary Marketplace (R. R. Bowker).

Photographer's Market (Writer's Digest Books).

Writer's Market (Writer's Digest Books).

CHAPTER NINE

The Self-Employed History Buff

Profiting from the Past

Business-minded history buffs who want to be their own bosses and pursue their love of history have successfully ventured into a variety of endeavors. In doing so, they've established businesses satisfying not only their own interests but also fulfilling the needs of other history buffs. In this chapter, you will meet a horse-drawn carriage tour operator in Charleston, South Carolina; an antique and collectibles dealer in Ithaca, New York; an auctioneer from Athens, Pennsylvania; a vintage clothing expert in Fort Lauderdale, Florida; and the proprietors of a historic inn on Nantucket Island.

Close-Up: Carriage Tour Operator

"There's nothing better than a good mule; there's nothing worse than a bad one," says Tom Doyle, owner of the Palmetto Carriage Works, a horse- and mule-drawn carriage tour company in Charleston, South Carolina. "The thing about the bad ones, though, is that they don't hide it very well. I can spend an afternoon with a mule and know whether or not it's going to work. A horse will go by something ninety-nine times as if it weren't there, but on the hundredth time, the time you're not paying attention, the horse will absolutely freak out. Mules are much easier to train."

And if anyone should know the characteristics of mules, it's Tom Doyle. He has built up his tour business and now employs several dozen people, owns two stables right in the heart of the city, and has more than twenty carriages, plus horses and mules.

"The fellow who began the business started off with just the frame of an old farm wagon," Tom recalls. "He built some seats and a roof on top of it. He also had a carriage from the Jack Daniels Brewery, and he picked up a few old carriages from auctions. But they're not really built heavy duty enough for the kind of work we use them for, and they're too small. It's hard to find an antique carriage that will carry six or sixteen people. Because of that, we began designing our own carriages."

Tom employs one person who does nothing but build carriages. He also has a full barn staff, an office manager, a bookkeeper, a secretary, a ticket collector, and drivers who also double as grooms. But everyone is also a licensed tour guide.

"The key to doing well in the carriage business," Tom explains, "is when the business is here, you've got to be able to handle it, and when it's not here, you have to be able to get real small. We're very seasonal."

Tom Doyle moved to Charleston from Massachusetts to study at the Citadel. When he finished with his bachelor's degree in history, he looked around for work he would enjoy. But most of the things he liked to do didn't pay enough money to support a family, so he was often forced to hold down two jobs. Out of this moonlighting, he discovered the Palmetto Carriage Works and started there as a part-time carriage driver–cum–tour guide. Within a year, however, he had graduated to full-time status and was working sixty to seventy hours a week. When the original owner decided it was time to retire in 1982, he offered the business to Tom.

"I didn't have a dime at the time," Tom admits, "but he gave me such a good deal, I was able to go out and find some other people who were willing to invest, and I put together a little group of silent partners."

But it's possible to start small in this business, Tom maintains. You don't need an office or a ticket collector or a fleet of carriages. With an investment of about $6,000—for the carriage, the tack, the animal, and various permits—you can position yourself in a place that's visible to tourists, perhaps outside a visitor's information center or near a popular place to stay or visit.

"It's a see-and-do thing," says Tom. "The carriages themselves are the best advertising. Tourists will ask the driver, 'Hey, how do I get on one of these?'" The real bread and butter of the business is the walk-up tourist.

"But to make it work, you have to live the business," Tom warns. "You have to be out there driving every day, making friends and getting to know everyone. Then word of mouth will get you going."

Tom also markets his business to the big hotels in town and the meeting planners and has found his niche with large groups. "People come into town for a conference or some other event, and they might want to do an off-premises function, maybe have dinner at a historic building. I tell them, 'Well, here's what we'll do. We'll pick you up in carriages and transport you there.'"

Tom also runs a free shuttle service with his 1934 antique Ford bus. He moves his customers from the visitor's center to his starting point.

Tom's tours are an hour long and cover twenty blocks of the old city. Drivers provide a nonstop narration about Charleston's history, architecture, gardens, people, and points of interest.

"As opposed to a motorized tour, our drivers can turn and talk to the people and make eye contact," Tom says. "It's a leisurely business. While you're waiting for the carriage to fill up, you chat with the passengers. To have a really great tour, you need to get to know your customers. And tourists are great to deal with because 99.9 percent of them are in a good mood. They're on vacation, after all! When I take people on a carriage tour, everyone in the city benefits because I leave them so happy with Charleston, they're wanting to do more and to come back."

To have a successful business, you must love the city where you're set up, and you have to be an expert and know everything about its local history. "Good business sense is also important," Tom says, "and when you're the boss you have to monitor your drivers—the tour they give is the most important part. I occasionally pay strangers to ride and check out the drivers."

Tom is convinced that it's more than a job, it's a lifestyle. "You get to work with the animals, which I really like; you can bring your children to work, and all the neighborhood kids come around the stables to help out and get free rides. You have to do a good job. You're not only representing yourself, you're representing the whole city."

If you can find an Amish settlement, you'll be able to find carriages and farm wagons for sale. There are large settlements in Pennsylvania, Indiana, Ohio, and Tennessee. To help locate these settlements, write or call the state's department of tourism, which will be able to direct you.

Close-Up: Antique Dealer

"If you scratch a dealer, you'll find a collector underneath," reveals Adam Perl, proprietor of Pastimes, an antiques and collectibles shop in Ithaca, New York. "Many of us have gone into business just to finance our collecting habits." Adam's own collecting habit began in the seventh grade when a classmate brought a book to school called *Cash for Your Coins*. But even if that hadn't happened, it's unlikely the collecting bug would have passed Adam by. He grew up surrounded by art and antiques; his mother is an art historian who worked at the Museum of Modern Art in New York, the Andrew Dickson White Museum at Cornell, and the Smithsonian's Hirshhorn

Museum. His father was a writer, and both parents were serious antique collectors.

Surprisingly, Adam had never been to an auction until he was a young adult. He had just rented an unfurnished apartment when he found out about a country auction being held nearby.

"I was instantly hooked. I spent $100 and filled my van three times. I furnished my entire apartment, with items left over to spare. The early seventies was a golden age of buying, when wonderful three- and four-generation estates were being broken up all over the country, but especially in the Northeast. There wasn't much of an antique market in any field then—you could buy anything for the proverbial song in those days."

With no thought of turning it into a business at that time, Adam began frequenting auctions for the fun of it. He'd go out with $5 or $10 in his pocket and come home with treasures. "I kept doing it over and over again, until I felt I had much more than I could fit in my apartment," he recalls. "I realized from seeing people's setups at flea markets that they had an organized system of pricing and that they generally specialized in a particular area, such as knives or dolls. I learned that if I took the things I bought and cleaned them up a bit—polished the brass, refinished the wood, and stove-blacked the iron—that I could actually sell them for more than I had paid for them. I had my first garage sale and made a little money on it. It wasn't much of a step from that to connect with New York City and the contacts I had there."

He talked to several dealers and tried to learn from people who were sympathetic and who would teach him. "At the time, the world of antiques was pretty much a mystery; there was this arcane underground where people wouldn't reveal their secrets or knowledge to anyone," Adam says.

Adam found his sympathetic antique dealers at American Hurrah, which is now a well-known shop run by Joel and Kate Kopp, specializing in quilts and photographic images. "The Kopps were very forthcoming and didn't hold anything back," he recalls. "They taught me that you should try to double your money. You don't always do it, or sometimes you do better, but that's what you aim for. They taught me how to judge the condition of an item and how to develop and trust your own taste. They also helped to bail me out when I made mistakes.

"I became a 'picker,' a term in the industry for a wholesaler. The picker, during his antique hunting expeditions, tries to pick out the one great item out of the ten thousand he sees. I would actually buy retail at shops in upstate New York, perhaps finding a quilt, beautifully made and in excellent condition, for $25 to $50. I would then take it to the city and sell it for double the purchase price.

"The Kopps had taught me to look for the fine cotton quilts that were hand stitched with good colors and good patterns and early nineteenth-century materials. I had bought a quilt at a garage sale for $4 but it didn't meet any of those criteria. It was thick, heavy wool, twentieth century, rather ugly. But still, there was something about it that was really striking. It had a man's wool tank-top bathing suit stitched into it, complete with its Sears Roebuck label. I took this to New York, but the Kopps didn't think much of it. But they were always very nice to me; they bought the quilt for $12, and I was relieved. Later they turned around and were able to sell it for $50. This quilt was sold many times and eventually ended up in the Louvre Museum in Paris as an important example of early twentieth-century American folk art. Anybody who's been in business has made mistakes from time to time. Incidents like this can happen to the best of us."

Starting on a Shoestring

Adam opened his first shop in 1973 with just $400. A condemned high school had just been bought by an architect who remodeled it and converted it into a lively arcade of shops and boutiques called the DeWitt Building. Adam rented an unpretentious hole-in-the-wall for $125 a month plus one month's rent as a security deposit. The landlord gave him some paint, and he bought a huge old machine-made oriental rug for $1. "The rug had several feet missing in the corner. I spent another $1 and bought a big overstuffed chair to cover the hole. After the $2 that I spent on decor, I had $148 left for merchandise," he says.

Adam left the business for a few years, then returned in 1978 to open his current shop, Pastimes. "This is one of the best businesses to get into on little or no capital," he says. "You don't need any particular expertise or any particular degree. You do need to have some stock and a couple of tables and table coverings. And then you can hit the flea markets. You can still find perfectly good flea markets where you can set up for $10 to $25. Later you can graduate to a little bit higher-caliber show, whose fees might be from $35 to $100. A lot of people just do shows. It's the exception actually having a retail shop. You're tied down and have the overhead.

"Many people get started in this business as they're heading toward retirement. They ease into it the last five or ten years of their working careers and then do it as a retirement business to supplement their pensions and social security income.

"And, it's a recession-resistant business. When times are hard, antiques are a better buy than new items. People are shopping more carefully, and even noncollectors who just want to get good practical furniture, tools, or gifts will turn to antiques."

Adam is a firm believer that in this business, the less money you have, the better. "I knew a young man who had inherited $50,000. This was many years ago when that was really a lot of money. He went out and bought every exquisite piece of furniture he could find. I remember at the auctions I was very jealous; he could outbid everybody. He opened up a shop with all those beautiful things, but he couldn't sell them because he'd paid too much for them. You have to develop through experience knowledge of what the market will bear. There's no substitute for the actual buying and selling of merchandise to learn about the market and pricing. There are thousands of antique price guides, but this is something you can't really learn by the book. It's best to get into it gradually, go to a lot of antique shows and shops, compare prices, do your homework."

And you have to be careful about where you buy your merchandise, Adam warns. It's vital to make sure the auctioneers and dealers are reputable. "There's a great deal of dishonesty in the business," Adam admits. "A dealer might misrepresent an item's condition or authenticity. It's easy to get caught. Fairly recently a local dealer of questionable repute came across a big stash of mint-condition German lithographs that were reported to be from the turn of the century. We'd never seen anything like it—there are certain processes you just can't duplicate, and this was one of them. The dealers were scarfing them up for $7 to $10 apiece. We found out they were repros, but not before a lot of us got stung.

"And seventeen years ago I was selling some red-colored Fiestaware, a very popular deco dinnerware made by Homer Laughlin in the thirties, forties, and fifties. It turned out to be radioactive. Some of the glazes had been made with uranium."

Choose Your Specialty

There are probably more than ten thousand branches in the antiques and collectibles business. Some collectors specialize in nothing but actual items used in the Civil War. You can take any particular area of your interest, whether it be local history, silver making, the history of advertising, woodworking, tools, lace making, or photography, and turn that one area into a whole specialty and a whole business.

"Look for an area you love," Adam advises, "and learn more about it and concentrate in it. I specialize in about five or six areas I happen to have a particular love and feeling for—antique buttons, costume jewelry from the Victorian era through the forties, 1910 postcards, fountain pens, sterling silver, and antique beads. We also carry some oak furniture, glassware, and photography. Pastimes is relatively small, but it looks like a well-organized and cleaned-up flea market."

Adam loves what he's doing, always chasing after the next bargain, enjoying the wonderful thrill of the hunt, that feeling you get looking for treasures and bargains. "It keeps you excited and fueled up when you're unloading your van in the cold rain or you're stuck in the mud at an auction." Adam notes that the rise of the Internet, specifically eBay, has been a boon to the antiques business.

Close-Up: Auctioneer

"I have this nice oak rolltop desk, how about a five hundred dollar bid, get five hundred, get five hundred, get two and a half, start us off, give us a hundred, give a hundred . . ." is part of the chant you'll hear from auctioneer Jim Ridolfi, owner of the Aspon Trading Company in Troy, Pennsylvania. "Everyone has a chant, and everyone develops their own," Jim says. "I try not to use too many words—the people won't understand you. What they're listening for is the numbers. You learn a basic method at auctioneer training school, and then you take it and refine it and make it into your own."

Education and Training

Training programs can run from two weeks to three or four months, depending on your state's requirements. While in training, auctioneers also study communications skills, the law as applied to auctioneers, marketing and advertising, auction management, appraisal, and selling real estate.

Different states have different licensing laws: some states have none at all, but some are very rigorous with what they require.

Many auctioneers go through various national auctioneering schools; the best-known one is the Missouri Auction School. But it's important to check first which schools your state will accept. Pennsylvania, for example, only accepts training through the two schools in Pennsylvania. The best thing to do is contact your state licensing board and find out what it requires, then write or call the National Auctioneers Association (listed in Appendix A) to find the appropriate training.

Like Jim Ridolfi, many auctioneers are also antique dealers. Jim specializes in old phonographs and radios and has a particular love for mid- to late-nineteenth-century items. In addition to antiques, auctioneers also handle household items, livestock, and real estate.

Jim became an auctioneer in 1992. He advertises his services in newspapers and has made contacts with other antique dealers, estate attorneys, and will executors.

Auctioneers hold their events indoors in hotel ballrooms or outside in a farmer's field or an estate's backyard. They work on a percentage basis, earning between 15 and 30 percent of the price of each item sold.

In addition to the auctioneer, there are other employment possibilities working in and around auctions:

Runners move the items for sale from the holding area to the stage.

Floor managers supervise the runners, let them know which items are going up next, and take care of any other details so that the auctioneer is not distracted.

Clerks make a record of the proceedings and handle the numbering of lots and bidders.

Cashiers collect the money.

Security guards watch over the sold items while they're waiting to be picked up.

Caterers provide the refreshments for the audience and staff.

Advertisers and marketers help the auctioneer inform the public about his or her services and particular auction events.

Catalogers work with large estates, organizing the items and taking precise inventories.

Appraisers help authenticate and place dollar values on particular items.

Furniture refinishers and restorers, while not usually working directly with an auction, find work with dealers or private individuals giving life back to old or damaged items.

Flea market and antique show organizers put on the big events that attract thousands of people. They handle every detail, including advertising, allocating space, and collecting fees.

Close-Up: Vintage Clothing Specialist

Most children love to play dress-up, and Mary Ptak, owner of Jezebel, a vintage clothing shop in Fort Lauderdale, Florida, was no exception. "I wanted to spend all my time in people's attics," Mary confesses. "I was mainly interested in finding old-style clothing. When I was in college in the sixties, I would just literally knock on strangers' doors and ask them if I could clean out their attics. In those days, they were usually delighted for you to do that."

But times have changed, and people are much more aware of the treasures they might have stored away. "Gone are the days when you could pick up something for twenty-five cents or less," Mary says.

Mary has been in business since 1986. Over the years she has managed to build up an international clientele, including collectors from Japan, Germany, and England. "Our customers are an eclectic mix of people," Mary says. "People from England and Japan have been buying up everything they can find from the fifties. Our serious collectors tend to buy clothes from the thirties through the fifties—Joan Crawford, Great Gatsby, and Garbo styles with big padded shoulders and lots of sparkly glitz. Lilli Ann suits from the forties and fifties are popular now, too. They're extremely classy looking, nipped in at the waist with flaring peplums. Some of our customers are Victorian period collectors, but most people now want the article they're buying to be useful—they want to be able to wear it.

"Local kids are demanding sixties and seventies garments. The kids even want the polyester nik-nik shirts from the sixties—foul-looking things, but they're popular now. The kids are always a little more savvy than the general public, and they start fashion trends with their regular street clothes. I used to be able to buy what I liked; now I have to think in terms of my customers' needs."

Jezebel carries clothes ranging in price from $5 for an Indian cotton gauze blouse from the 1960s to a $2,000 Schaparelli gown. Mary also handles rentals, outfits murder mystery events, and has supplied the costumes for several major television shows and motion pictures, including "Key West," *Cape Fear*, and *Wrestling Ernest Hemingway*.

Mary travels all over the country to look for just the right pieces. She also has built up a network of people who ship her good finds.

"I learned what was collectible from being in the business a long time," Mary explains. "You have to have a good eye to pick what people want, and you have to change with the times— trends are constantly changing, and you can't always be buying the same things."

For anyone considering a similar business, Mary cautions that it is important to buy clothes that are in excellent condition, unless it's something that's really ancient and people would expect to be damaged. "And you also need a huge amount of stock. When I started out I had very little, but I took consignments then, and because I'm a fanatic shopper, it didn't take long to build it up."

She has also managed to build a first-class reputation. "I make an effort to pay people what they deserve for their merchandise—it's one of the reasons I've been so successful," Mary says.

Jezebel is a classic example of laughing all the way to the bank. In 1986, no one would give her a business loan. "They didn't think I'd make it," Mary says with just a hint of righteous indignation in her voice.

Mary is kept very busy. The one thing she doesn't have time to do anymore is hunt through people's attics. These days she can hire other people to do that.

Close-Up: Historic-Inn Proprietor

Many entrepreneurial history buffs have been caught up in a popular movement throughout the country—restoring and refurbishing historic homes and converting them into country inns, guest houses, and bed-and-breakfast establishments. Nantucket, Massachusetts, is filled with such historic homes, including an inn once owned by Roger and Mary Schmidt.

A Bit of History

The name *Nantucket* is a Native American word meaning "faraway land," and though this crescent-shaped island is only thirty miles off the coast of Massachusetts, it is, indeed, set apart with an Old World flavor all its own. Ferries transport visitors and residents back and forth between the island and the town of Hyannis on Cape Cod. Stepping off that ferry is like taking a step back in time to an age gone by.

Settled in 1659 (the Nine Original Purchasers, as they were called, gained possession from the English for the sum of thirty pounds and two beaver hats), the island prospered well into the mid-1800s as a major whaling port. But the invention of kerosene, an encroaching sandbar blocking the harbor, and the lure of the California Gold Rush all contributed to a quick demise. Not too much later, Americans began the now deeply ingrained tradition of summer vacations, and Nantucket was rediscovered. Business-minded homemakers turned their stately houses into guest inns or restaurants, and a new breed of fisher emerged to supply the "summer people" with Nantucket's bounty of shellfish: littleneck and cherrystone clams, quahogs, mussels, and the famous succulent bay scallops.

Today tourism still supports the seven thousand or so year-round residents (the summer population blossoms to nearly forty thousand each year), but the character of the island hasn't changed much through the years. Though pleasure boats have replaced the old wooden whaling vessels, the original Quaker homes, simple but sturdy dwellings, and the perfectly preserved Georgian, Federal, and Greek revival–style houses still stand in orderly ranks along cobblestoned Main Street and the other winding lanes and crisscrossing pathways of Nantucket Town.

Stroll down any narrow byway and take a peek into postage-stamp gardens filled with flowering rhododendron, azaleas, and other perennials. Some of the houses are impressive mansions, the legacy of the wealth-producing whaling industry. Others are small dollhouses with geranium-filled planter boxes sitting below lacy-curtained, leaded-glass windows.

A glimpse inside any of the homes reveals Old World mahogany antiques—carved sea chests and canopied or sleigh-back beds, many with shiny brass or even solid silver fixtures. White wicker rockers grace wooden porches, and widow's walks curve around under cedar-shake roof shingles.

The Nantucket Historical Association has a strong influence, and strict building codes are enthusiastically adhered to by residents. Though other tourist spots are often marred by lines of fast-food stands and high-rise hotels, no intrusive golden arches or glaring neon signs are allowed on the island. Even the gas stations are disguised, their red brick structures blending perfectly with their surroundings. So aesthetically pleasing is the island that American architects repeatedly vote Nantucket as the only "perfect ten" in the country.

Architecture and history buffs will discover, for a start, the Old Mill; the Jethro Coffin House, considered the oldest house on the island; and the Whaling Museum, as well as all the other designated landmarks. In fact, the entire town of Nantucket has been included as a district on the National Register of Historic Places.

Many of Nantucket's historic homes are now open to the public as museums, and others have become established as quaint and comfortable guest houses and inns.

The Inn at 18 Gardner Street

Roger and Mary Schmidt's inn was called simply the 18 Gardner Street Inn, on Nantucket Island. Although it is a private home now, the Schmidts operated their inn for many years. The colonial-style house, which is on the historical walking tour, was originally built in 1835 by Captain Robert Joy. The sea captain took the proceeds of his last whaling excursion and built the house to retire in. Since then, the home was owned by several different families. In the 1940s, the property was converted to a lodging house with six or seven rooms. The next family that purchased the inn installed bathrooms in the rooms and ran it as a bed-and-breakfast.

The Schmidts acquired the inn in 1988. The building is a traditional square box shape with a pitched roof and an ell in the back where the kitchen was added in the late 1800s. In front, there's a center door with original hand-rolled glass windows on each side. A typical Nantucket friendship staircase graces the front door, with steps on either side meeting at the landing at the top. Weathered cedar shakes (which, along with the famous Nantucket fog, help to contribute to the island's other nickname, the Grey Lady) and a large widow's walk complete the picture of an elegant sea captain's mansion.

Spread through the inn's two stories and finished third-floor attic were twelve guest rooms that the Schmidts had furnished with pencil-post, canopied, and four-poster beds and antique mahogany or cherry dressers and nightstands. All of the rooms were airy; many were spacious suites, most with fireplaces.

Roger and Mary and their two children occupied a two-bedroom apartment in the finished basement. During the first two years they owned the inn, the Schmidts completely refurnished it. In the third and fourth years, they started doing massive restoration to the guest rooms. They took all the wallpaper down and repaired the dozens of cracks they discovered in the plaster. They upgraded the bathrooms and, keeping the period appearance to the bedrooms, rewallpapered with pastels and satin wall coverings. They completely gutted the kitchen and replaced it with a new commercial kitchen so they could serve guests a full breakfast. And, as so often happens in old houses, they discovered a beautiful fireplace hidden for years behind one of the plaster walls. Every three years or so, the exterior of the house gets a new paint job.

One thing the Schmidts avoided was putting up new walls. They specifically chose an inn that wouldn't require massive reconstruction work. From experience, they learned that putting up sheet rock can get unbelievably expensive and complicated when dealing with commercial building codes. Because the property had been licensed for so many years as an inn, they didn't have to be relicensed, although they did have to get an annual license through the local building inspector.

Background

The Schmidts are originally from Springfield, in western Massachusetts. They honeymooned on Nantucket in 1977 and fell in love with the island. They started visiting three and four times a year. But when they started hunting for property to buy, it soon became obvious that the selling prices were way out of their reach. Roger explains:

"In the early eighties, property on Nantucket skyrocketed. I was in the electronics field, Mary worked in a photography lab, and the dream of owning a summer home got pushed aside because of economics. We went to the nearby island of Martha's Vineyard because we'd heard there were good buys there. We ended up finding some property there and got into the real estate business. We bought a mariner's home and completely restored it and turned it into a small, five-bedroom inn, and then we developed some other pieces of property there as well. This was all happening while we were still considering Springfield as our main residence. Eventually we sold it all off and came back to Nantucket in a much better financial condition to buy our current property.

"We had an innkeeper running 18 Gardner Street for us for two years, but we almost went bankrupt because of mismanagement. So, in April of 1990, we moved to the island permanently and took over running the inn. Business then took off like a cannonball. As terrible as this may sound, anybody who gets into this business and thinks they will succeed by serving the greatest cup of coffee and greeting every guest with a warm smile is totally wrong. It's not enough. You have to sell your property to a person on the other end of the phone. Unfortunately for that person, he doesn't know what he's getting. He can't see it and touch it. So through written advertisements in major newspapers such as the *Boston Globe* and the *New York Times*, and through verbal communications, you have to get across to your potential guests what your facilities are. Then when they come, you can give them the greatest cup of coffee and the warmest smile.

"But that's still not enough. You have to understand your guests' needs and try to meet them. For example, we listened to our guests and learned that it was an inconvenience for them to have to walk downtown to pick up their rented bicycles. So we bought bicycles and provided them to our guests free of charge. We also learned that in the autumn, it could be a long, cold walk back from town, so that's when we made sure all our fireplaces were working. That kept the fall business coming in. Again, we listened and learned that guests would like a little more than a muffin and coffee for breakfast, so we got a food-service permit and offered a full meal in the morning. We also provided dock-side shuttle service from the ferry to the inn, picnic baskets, beach blankets, and ice coolers. We did what we could to make our guests happy. This helped substantially to build our word-of-mouth referral business.

"A lot of people want to live out their romantic dream by retiring to an idyllic spot such as Nantucket and running a bed-and-breakfast. But the first major mistake they make is when they use the word *retiring*. There's nothing retiring, or romantic, about operating an inn. You have to work very hard.

"From April 1 to November 30, my day was primarily involved with taking reservations, handling problems, and delegating responsibilities to our staff of five. During the winter, we involved ourselves with marketing, interior design, and restoration. We were always busy."

Financial Considerations

The Schmidts have since closed the inn and converted the house to a private home, but Roger learned over the years how to handle the financial aspects of inn proprietorship. He says:

"In 1988, we paid $850,000 for our historic inn, and at the time, that was a good price. The property dropped in value to $600,000 in the next two years, but because of the restoration and the steady clientele we built up, our property, and our business, was worth slightly more than $1 million before we closed the inn.

"Our rooms were full about one hundred days of the year, and we were aiming to have full occupancy every weekend through the off-season months. The inn was an upscale one, and our high-season rates ranged from $140 to $170 a night. But our monthly operating expenses and our mortgage payments were very high, too.

"Nantucket, of course, is a small and very expensive island. There are many areas in the country where you could pick up a small house or an established inn for around $100,000.

"Whatever the value, the trick is to have an understanding of real estate financing and to try to be a little creative. In our case, we put very little down; the owner was willing to hold back a second mortgage. Another alternative is to lease with an option to buy. We did that with the property adjoining ours, which added five more guest rooms to book.

"But I would advise starting out with a property with just three or four guest rooms. It's a very risky business, and there's a high burnout and turnover rate. Sometimes the dream can turn into a nightmare. You can't treat it as a dream. You have to treat it as a business."

For More Information

Magazines can help the self-employed history buff feel connected in the field. Try *Antique Trader*, *Maine Antique Digest*, or *Newtown Bee*. You might also look for the following books:

How to Start and Run a Bed & Breakfast Inn, by Ripley Hotch and Carl Glassman (Stackpole Books). Covers buying the right inn, attracting guests, and estimating costs and profitability.

Sotheby's Caring for Antiques, edited by Mette Tang Simpson and Michael Huntley (Simon & Schuster). A guide to handling, cleaning, displaying, and restoring antiques.

Other Jobs for History Buffs

T his chapter describes additional jobs that may be of interest to history buffs. These include education and the "ologies"—anthropology, paleontology, and geology. These pursuits require additional academic training, including university degrees ranging from bachelor's all the way up to doctorates.

Those dedicated to following these career paths would benefit from further exploration into these diverse and interesting fields. There are many good books available on-line or at your local library or bookstore in the career section that will provide greater detail on your particular area of interest.

Here are a few of these employment possibilities not covered in previous chapters.

Education

Teachers must have a special talent; they carry a weighty responsibility. How they present their subjects will affect their students' attitudes toward history for a lifetime. A good teacher will know how to make history come alive and can show its importance to our lives today and for our future.

History courses are generally taught all throughout elementary, middle, and secondary schools. A teacher would need at least a bachelor's degree in history or history education.

To teach at the college level, a master's degree would be required—and in many cases, a doctorate. At the graduate level, teachers would need to specialize in a particular area such as American civilization or European history.

Educators also work in museums, presenting programs to the public and participating on curatorial teams to make sure the information being presented in exhibits is easily accessible to the audience.

Some private organizations, such as the Crow Canyon Archaeological Center, also employ educators to provide orientation information and training to participants.

Educators can find work with historical societies or preservation boards as information officers or in public relations.

Salaries for Educators

Median annual earnings of elementary and secondary school teachers range from $33,590 to $37,890, the lowest 10 percent earns $19,710 to $24,390, and the top 10 percent earns $53,720 to $70,030.

According to the American Federation of Teachers, beginning teachers with bachelor's degrees earn an average of $25,700. Private school teachers generally earn less than public school teachers.

In some schools, teachers receive extra pay for coaching sports and working with students in extracurricular activities. Some teachers earn extra income during the summer working in the school system or in other jobs.

Median annual earnings of college and university faculty are about $46,630. The middle 50 percent earns between $33,390 and $71,360. The lowest 10 percent earns less than $23,100; the highest 10 percent earns more than $90,360.

Earnings vary according to faculty rank, type of institution, geographic area, and field. According to a recent survey by the

American Association of University Professors, salaries for full-time faculty average $56,300. By rank, the average for professors is $72,700; associate professors, $53,200; assistant professors, $43,800; instructors, $33,400; and lecturers, $37,200.

Faculty in four-year institutions earn higher salaries, on the average, than those in two-year schools. Average salaries for faculty in public institutions—$55,900—are lower than those for private independent institutions—$63,500—but higher than those for religiously affiliated private colleges and universities—$49,400.

In fields with high-paying nonacademic alternatives—notably medicine and law but also engineering and business, among others—earnings exceed these averages. In others, such as the humanities, history, and education, they are lower.

Some faculty members have significant earnings, in addition to a base salary, that they receive for consulting, teaching additional courses, researching, writing for publication, or other employment.

The "Ologies"

Anthropology

Anthropology, the study of human beings, has four subdivisions: archaeology (which was discussed in Chapter 7), cultural anthropology, physical anthropology, and linguistics.

Cultural anthropology looks at all of the manifestations of culture, including early civilizations that are now extinct, up through groups of people that exist today. *Ethnology* is a branch of cultural anthropology that looks at the historical development of cultures, the distinguishing characteristics of the different races, and the similarities and differences between cultures.

Physical anthropology studies early people and evolution. *Linguistics* is the science of language and how it develops. The field of linguistics is further divided into historical, descriptive, and applied linguistics.

Anthropologists work in academic settings or live in the field among different groups and indigenous cultures.

Paleontology

Paleontologists are concerned with the forms of life that existed in earlier periods. They study fossilized plants, animals, and bones and find work in academic settings or with natural history museums.

Geology

Geology is the science concerned with the physical history of the earth. Geologists study rocks and the physical changes the earth has undergone. In addition to teaching, geologists work for engineering firms and oil companies and with architects and archaeologists.

For More Information

The following books cover, in greater detail, some of the career paths mentioned in this chapter as well as others that may appeal to history buffs. All were published by VGM Career Books.

Careers in Education, by Roy A. Edelfelt

Great Jobs for Anthropology Majors, by Blythe Camenson

Great Jobs for Geology Majors, by Blythe Camenson

Great Jobs for History Majors, by Julie Ann DeGalan and Stephen E. Lambert

In addition to reading as much as you can about the careers that interest you, you should talk to people working in the different fields, carefully prepare your resume, and then present yourself to those who are in the position to hire new employees. Whether you're transforming your favorite hobby into a dream job or are committed to pursuing an academic interest, you will find a history-related career to be fulfilling on many levels. Good luck!

Professional Associations

Y ou can use the following list of associations as a valuable resource guide in locating additional information about specific careers. Many of the organizations publish newsletters listing job and internship opportunities, and still others offer employment placement services to members.

Internet addresses are listed for associations with websites. A few clicks will bring you to extensive career information.

Advisory Council on Historic Preservation
1100 Pennsylvania Avenue NW
Washington, DC 20004

American Anthropological Association (AAA)
American Anthropological Placement Service
4350 North Fairfax Drive, Suite 640
Arlington, VA 22203
www.aaanet.org

American Association for Museum Volunteers
6307 Hardy Drive
McLean, VA 22101

American Association for State and Local History
1717 Church Street
Nashville, TN 37203
www.aaslh.org

American Association of Christian Schools
P.O. Box 1097
Independence, MO 64051
www.aacs.org

American Association of Colleges for Teacher Education
One Dupont Circle NW, Suite 610
Washington, DC 20036

American Association for Higher Education
One Dupont Circle NW, Suite 360
Washington, DC 20036
www.aahe.org

American Association of Museums
1575 Eye Street NW, Suite 400
Washington, DC 20005
www.aam-us.org

American Craft Council
Information Center
72 Spring Street
New York, NY 10012
www.craftcouncil.org

American Ethnological Society (AES)
Member Services
American Anthropological Association
4350 North Fairfax Drive, Suite 640
Arlington, VA 22203
www.aaanet.org

American Federation of Teachers
555 New Jersey Ave NW
Washington, DC 20001
www.aft.org

American Historical Association
400 A Street SE
Washington, DC 20003
www.theaha.org

American Institute of Architects
1735 New York Avenue NW
Washington, DC 20006
www.aia.org

American Library Association
50 East Huron Street
Chicago, IL 60611
www.ala.org

American Sociological Association
1307 New York Avenue NW, Suite 700
Washington, DC 20005
www.asanet.org

American Society of Church History
P.O. Box 8517
Red Bank, NJ 07701
www.churchhistory.org

Archaeological Conservancy
5301 Central Avenue NE, Suite 1218
Albuquerque, NM 87108
www.americanarchaeology.com

Archaeological Institute of America
656 Beacon Street, Fourth Floor
Boston, MA 02215
www.archaeological.org

Archaeology Section
American Anthropological Association
4350 North Fairfax Drive, Suite 640
Arlington, VA 22203
www.aaanet.org

Association for Art History
Henry Radford Hope School of Fine Arts
Fine Arts 124
Indiana University—Bloomington
Bloomington, IN 47405
www.indiana.edu/~aah

Association for Gravestone Studies
278 Main Street, Suite 207
Greenfield, MA 01301
www.gravestonestudies.org

Association of American Colleges and Universities
1818 R Street NW
Washington, DC 20009
www.aacu-edu.org

Association of Living Historical Farms and Agricultural
   Museums
8774 Route 45 NW
North Bloomfield, OH 44450
www.alhfam.org

Association of Professional Genealogists
P.O. Box 40393
Denver, CO 80204
www.apgen.org

Society for Archaeological Sciences
Office of the General Secretary
SAS, Department of Anthropology
University of California
Riverside, CA 92521
www.wisc.edu/larch/sas/sas.htm

Society for Historical Archaeology
P.O. Box 30446
Tucson, AZ 85751
www.sha.org

Society of American Archivists
527 South Wells Street, Fifth Floor
Chicago, IL 60607
www.archivists.org

Society of Architectural Historians
1365 North Astor Street
Chicago, IL 60610
www.sah.org

Living History Museums

W hat follows is a sampling of the thousands of living history museums located throughout the country. Some have websites that list current employment opportunities. Contact those that interest you directly for more information.

Canadian Museum of Civilization
100 Laurier Street
P.O. Box 3100 Station B
Hull, QU J8X 4H2
Canada
www.civilization.ca

Charlton Park
2545 South Charlton Park Road
Hastings, MI 49058
www.flint.lib.mi.us/fpl/resources/reenactment/livhis_centers.html

Clear Creek History Park
c/o Astor House Museum
822 Twelfth Street
Golden, CO 80401
www.web-span.com/fastpart/ccrp2.html

Colonial Williamsburg
P.O. Box 1776
Williamsburg, VA 23187
www.history.org

El Rancho de Las Golondrinas
334 Los Pinos Road
Santa Fe, NM 87505
www.golondrinas.org

Frontier Culture Museum
P.O. Box 810
Staunton, VA 24402
www.frontiermuseum.org

Genesee Country Village & Museum
Flint Hill Road
Mumford, NY 14511
www.gcv.org

Hancock Shaker Village
P.O. Box 927
Pittsfield, MA 01202
www.hancockshakervillage.org

Irish Village
P.O. Box 320
East Durham, NY 12423
www.irelandsvillage.com

Living History Farms
2600 Northwest 111th Street
Urbandale, IA 50322
www.lhf.org

Museum Village
1010 Route 17M
Monroe, NY 10950
www.fieldtrip.com/ny/47828247.htm

Mystic Seaport
P.O. Box 6000
75 Greenmanville Avenue
Mystic, CT 06355
www.mysticseaport.org

Lowell National Historical Park
67 Kirk Street
Lowell, MA 01852
www.nps.gov/lowe

Old Cowtown Museum
1871 Sim Park Drive
Wichita, KS 67203
www.old-cowtown.org

Old Salem
P.O. Box F, Salem Station
Winston-Salem, NC 27108
www.oldsalem.org

Old Sturbridge Village
One Old Sturbridge Village Road
Sturbridge, MA 01566
www.osv.org

Plimoth Plantation
P.O. Box 1620
Plymouth, MA 02360
www.plimoth.org

Pioneer Arizona Living History Museum
3901 West Pioneer Road
Phoenix, AZ 85086
www.pioneer-arizona.com

Rhinebeck Aerodrome Museum
P.O. Box 229
Rhinebeck, NY 12572
www.oldrhinebeck.org

St. Augustine's Spanish Quarter Village
Historic St. Augustine Preservation Board
P.O. Box 1987
St. Augustine, FL 32085
www.oldcity.com/spanishquarter

Stuhr Museum of the Prairie Pioneer
P.O. Box 1801
Grand Island, NE 68802
www.stuhrmuseum.org

Washington Irving Trail Museum
Route 1, Box 880
Ripley, OK 74062
www.cowboy.net/non-profit/irving

National Park Service Regional Offices

ALASKA REGION
National Park Service
2525 Gambell Street
Anchorage, AK 99503

PACIFIC NORTHWEST REGION
National Park Service
83 South King Street, #212
Seattle, WA 98104

WESTERN REGION
National Park Service
600 Harrison Street, #600
San Francisco, CA 94107

ROCKY MOUNTAIN REGION
National Park Service
P.O. Box 25287
Denver, CO 80225

SOUTHWEST REGION
National Park Service
P.O. Box 728
Santa Fe, NM 87501

MIDWEST REGION
National Park Service
1709 Jackson Street
Omaha, NE 68102

SOUTHEAST REGION
National Park Service
Richard B. Russell Federal
    Building
75 Spring Street SW
Atlanta, GA 30303

MID-ATLANTIC REGION
National Park Service
143 South Third Street
Philadelphia, PA 19106

NATIONAL CAPITAL REGION
National Park Service
1100 Ohio Drive SW
Washington, DC 20242

NORTH ATLANTIC REGION
National Park Service
15 State Street
Boston, MA 02109

Further Reading

1001 Things Everyone Should Know About American History, by J. A. Garraty (Doubleday).

The American Heritage Book of Great Historic Places (American Heritage Publishing Co., Inc.).

America Then & Now, edited by David Cohen (Harper San Francisco).

The Antiques Clinic: A Guide to Damage, Care, and Restoration, by James Fielden, Richard Garnier, Yukette Burt, Paul Davidson (Barron's Educational Series).

Directory of Historical Organizations in the United States and Canada, edited by Mary Bray Wheeler (American Association for State and Local History). This book is currently out of print, but used copies can be ordered through www.powells.com. It lists more than thirteen thousand historical and genealogical societies, museums, archives, and other history-related groups.

Furniture Care and Conservation, by Robert F. McGiffin (Association for State and Local History). Techniques for museums, dealers, and collectors on methods and products for preserving furniture.

Great Jobs for History Majors, by Julie Ann DeGalan and Stephen E. Lambert (VGM Career Books).

A Guide to Artifacts of Colonial America, by Ivor Noel Hume (Alfred A. Knopf).

Interpretation of Historic Sites, by William T. Alderson (Association for State and Local History). How to develop and conduct interpretive programs.

Introduction to Museum Work, by G. Ellis Burcaw (American Association for State and Local History). For museum workers worldwide. Covers collections, interpretation, educational programs, and exhibits.

A Living History Reader: Museums, by Jay Anderson (Altamira Press). An anthology of articles written about living history by museum interpreters and enthusiasts.

National Register of Historic Places, by the American Association for State and Local History, National Park Service, and National Conference of State Historic Preservation Officers. Listing of more than fifty thousand designations by the National Park Service as places worthy of preservation.

Past into Present: Effective Techniques for First-Person Historical Interpretation, by Stacy Flora Roth (University of North Carolina Press).

Peterson's Guide to Graduate and Professional Programs: An Overview (Peterson's Guides).

Recreating the Historic House Interior, by William Seale (American Association for State and Local History). This book is currently out of print, but used copies available from www.powells.com. It covers methods for restoration, researching, architectural decisions, floors, wall coverings, and lighting.

Chronicle Guidance Publications puts out a series of briefs explaining the following professions: anthropologists, archaeologists, criminologists, demographers, economists, genealogists, geographers, librarians, linguists, museum curators, political scientists, and sociologists. They can be ordered through:

Chronicle Guidance Publications, Inc.
66 Aurora Street
Moravia, NY 13118
www.chronicleguidance.com

Listings of State Historic Preservation Officers (SHPOs) are available from:

National Conference of SHPOs
Suite 332, Hall of the States
444 North Capitol Street
Washington, DC 20001

About the Author

Growing up in historic New England, Blythe Camenson became an avid history buff. Surrounded by red brick and ivy, Victorian gingerbread, and quaint and picturesque seaports and harbors, she developed an inevitable love of history.

Through her travels overseas in Europe and the Middle East, her interests broadened. She spent eight years working in the Persian Gulf, teaching English at various universities. Her many travel articles have appeared in both national and international publications.

In addition to extensive writing on the subject of careers—with more than four dozen books in print—she has also written several books to help new writers learn how to get published. *Your Novel Proposal: From Creation to Contract* (Writer's Digest Books), coauthored with Marshall J. Cook, has been particularly well received.

Camenson is also director of Fiction Writer's Connection (FWC), an organization dedicated to helping new writers improve their skills and learn the many steps involved in working toward publication. She maintains an informational website at www.fictionwriters.com and is a frequent speaker at national conferences and bookstores.

She earned her bachelor of arts degree with a double major in English and psychology from the University of Massachusetts in Boston and her master of education degree (M.Ed.), with a major in counseling, from Northeastern University, also in Boston.